THE NATIONAL INSTITUTE OF
ECONOMIC AND SOCIAL RESEARCH

Occasional Papers
XL

BRITAIN'S PRODUCTIVITY GAP

BRITAIN'S PRODUCTIVITY GAP

STEPHEN DAVIES

and

RICHARD E. CAVES

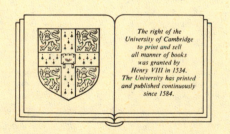

The right of the
University of Cambridge
to print and sell
all manner of books
was granted by
Henry VIII in 1534.
The University has printed
and published continuously
since 1584.

CAMBRIDGE UNIVERSITY PRESS

CAMBRIDGE

LONDON   NEW YORK   NEW ROCHELLE
MELBOURNE   SYDNEY

Published by the Press Syndicate of the University of Cambridge
The Pitt Building, Trumpington Street, Cambridge CB2 1RP
32 East 57th Street, New York, NY 10022, USA
10 Stamford Road, Oakleigh, Melbourne 3166, Australia

First published 1987

Printed in Great Britain at the University Press, Cambridge

British Library cataloguing in publication data

Davies, S. W.
Britain's productivity gap: a study based
on British and American industries, 1968–1977
1. Industrial productivity – Great
Britain – History – 20th century
2. Industrial productivity – United
States – History – 20th century
1. Title II. Caves, Richard
338.4'567'0941 HC260.152

Library of Congress cataloguing in publication data

Davies, S. W.
Britain's productivity gap.
Bibliography:
1. Industrial productivity – Great Britain.
2. Industrial productivity – United States. 1. Caves,
Richard E. II. Title.
HC260.152D38 1987 338'.06'0941 86–23261

ISBN 0 521 33464 0

SE

CONTENTS

List of tables   *page* viii
List of charts   ix
Preface   xiii
List of abbreviations   x

I   PRODUCTIVITY LEVELS IN BRITISH AND
   AMERICAN INDUSTRIES   I
   The statistical record   2
   Labour relations   4
     Strikes   5
     Restrictive rules   6
     Policy overtime   6
     Other resource costs   7
   Skills of management and labour   8
     Investment in human resources   10
   Sizes of companies and plants   11
     Sizes of companies   11
     Sizes of plants   13
     Concentration of producers   14
   Productivity constraints and their social context   14

2   RELATIVE INDUSTRIAL PRODUCTIVITY: AN
   ANALYTICAL FRAMEWORK   17
   The core neoclassical model   17
     Differences in production functions   20
     Measuring typical plant size   21
   Incorporating differences in human capital   23
   Impact of labour relations on productivity   24
     Direct and indirect costs of strikes   25
     Disruption to production lines   27
     Uncertainty   27
     The atmosphere of labour relations   28

3   DETERMINANTS OF RELATIVE EFFICIENCY   31
   Estimation of the neoclassical core model   31

Contents

Hypotheses relating to efficiency differences   35
    The managerial factor   36
    Labour relations   37
    Industrial organisation and competition   40
Statistical results   43
    Managerial factors   43
    Labour relations   44
    Industrial organisation and competition   47
    A complete econometric specification   48
Summary   49

4 PRODUCTIVITY, PRICES, MARKET STRUCTURE,
   AND INTERNATIONAL TRADE   51
Relative productivity as cause and effect   51
A simultaneous model – general structure   52
Statistical results   56
    Effect of changes in specification of extended
      model   59
    The extended system estimated for 1967/8   61
Summary   62

5 RELATIVE PRODUCTIVITY IN LARGE PLANTS   64
Descriptive analysis   64
Regression analyses of $VPW1$ and $VPW2$ 66
Summary   69

6 RELATIVE PRODUCTIVITY GROWTH   71
Some descriptive evidence   72
Framework for analysing comparative rates of productivity
growth   75
    Effect of declining employment   76
Were British industries catching up?   77
    Methods of modelling catch-up   77
    Results   78
    Simultaneous model   80
    Inter-industry differences in growth of efficiency 80
Summary   82

7 CONCLUSIONS AND POLICY IMPLICATIONS   84
Quantitative implications of findings on productivity
shortfall   84
    Inter-industry differences in productivity
      performance   84
    Implications for the overall gap   86
    Gains from attaining equality   87
    Gains from attaining best practice   90

Lessons for analysing productivity   92
Implications for policy   94
    Competition and business organisation   94
    Human capital   94
    Labour relations   95
    Policies toward adjustment and reallocation   95

APPENDIX I THE SAMPLE INDUSTRIES   98
Concordance of industries   98
Coverage of the sample   102
APPENDIX II VARIABLE DEFINITIONS AND DATA
SOURCES   104

Notes   112
References   122
Index   129

TABLES

1.1 Total factor productivity and its components, United   *page*
Kingdom, France, Germany, and Japan relative to
the United States   3

1.2 Comparative labour productivity, United Kingdom,
Germany, and United States, selected sectors, 1968
and 1977   4

3.1 Estimates of determinants of *VPW*, 1967/8 and 1977,
neoclassical core model   34

3.2 Explanations of strike activity (strikes per establishment) utilised to generate *BEL*, United Kingdom and
United States, 1967/8 and 1977   39

3.3 Tests of hypotheses concerning determinants of *VPW*,
1967/8 and 1977   46

3.4 Preferred results, full model of determinants of *VPW*,
1967/8 and 1977   47

4.1 Estimation of simultaneous system of relations, 1977   57

4.2 Determinants of *VPW* estimated by method of instrumental variables, with alternative specifications of imports and exports, 1977   60

4.3 Determinants of *VPW* estimated by method of instrumental variables, 1967/8, with alternative specifications of imports and exports   61

5.1 Determinants of *VPW*, large-plant and small-plant
sectors of matched United Kingdom and United
States manufacturing industries, 1967/8 and 1977   67

6.1 Descriptive statistics, measures of growth in output per
employee, total output, and employment, 61 matched
British and American industries, 1968–77   72

6.2 Decomposition of mean and variance of logarithms of
VPWG   73

6.3 Regressions of growth in net output per employee on
growth of net output, 61 matched British and American industries, 1968–77   74

6.4 Determinants of relative productivity growth, 61
matched UK/US industries   76

6.5 Determinants of relative productivity growth, 61 matched industries, including determinants of level of relative efficiency 79

6.6 Analysis of relative levels and growth rates of efficiency, 61 matched industries, 1967/8–1977 82

7.1 Matched UK/US industries with highest and lowest ratios of UK/US net output per head, 1977 85

7.2 Average difference between matched industries with highest and lowest relative net output per head in selected explanatory variables, 1977 86

7.3 'Best' ordinary least squares model of determinants of relative labour productivity, re-estimated for analysis of closing the productivity gap 89

7.4 Predicted percentage improvements in relative net output per head resulting from movement of exogenous variables, 1967/8 and 1977 90

A.1 The sample industries: a concordance between the United Kingdom and the United States standard industrial classifications 99

A.2 Coverage of the sample 102

SYMBOLS IN THE TABLES
. . . not available
——nil or negligible
n.a. not applicable

CHARTS

2.1 A diagrammatic representation of *EFF* 19

6.1 A diagrammatic representation of catching-up: growth in efficiency against initial efficiency 81

PREFACE

In recent years the National Institute has produced a number of Occasional Papers on various aspects of productivity in Britain: these have included studies involving detailed measurement of the productivity differential between Britain and its competitors in the Industrial and Services sector, case study analysis of the relationship between structure and productivity, and ongoing work highlights the important role of vocational training. In the rather more distant past, Rostas' *Comparative Productivity in British and American Industry* first established a NIESR concern with the 'productivity problem'.

We offer this study as a contribution to the series, whilst noting that methodologically it is somewhat different from these previous studies. Our work is based on a cross-section econometric explanation of the productivity differential between a large number of British manufacturing industries and their American counterparts. In the main we have worked with published data sources such as the Census of Production in both countries. The tradition of large-scale econometric modelling is, of course, well established in the wider literature on Industrial Organisation (although it has been applied only rarely to the special analysis of productivity). In our opinion it has much to offer: the capacity to evaluate a wide range of, sometimes conflicting, hypotheses within a consistent framework which can also encompass simultaneous relationships between variables (in this case, for example, trade structure and productivity). Equally however, it has its limitations: the focus tends to be an *average* relationship across industries; sometimes statistical results are open to alternative interpretations; and the research is only as good as the data upon which it is based.

Thus a study such as this one is no substitute for the careful *case study*, as in the above mentioned work on vocational training (an important subject, incidentally, which we have been unable to model within our methodology, not least because of the paucity of published data sources). Nor does it remove the need for painstaking research on the many thorny measurement problems in this area; indeed it underlines the importance of such research. In short, we urge the reader to view our contribution as complementary to those listed in our opening paragraph – as one of a series of studies which, when taken together, constitute a fairly broad research programme.

We have pitched our research, and the exposition of this book, at a level designed to interest both the academic economist and non-specialists concerned with the pressing problem of low British productivity, and policies aimed at its solution. In practice, this means that we have tried to develop our models and specifications wherever possible from a sound theoretical perspective, rather than *ad hoc* conjectures. At the same time, however, we have also tried to provide intuitive explanations and to avoid over-technical elaboration. We hope not to have fallen between two stools! We should like to thank the Harvard Business School for access to the P.I.C.A. database which has been the source of much of our American data.

The genesis of our work lies in an earlier paper by Dick Caves on *Productivity Differences among Industries* (in *Britain's Economic Performance*) in 1980. That paper provided an underlying methodology and set of hypotheses which have now been developed in this study. Shortly after the appearance of that paper, the National Institute encouraged us to join forces (Davies having earlier worked as consultant on one of the measurement studies referred to earlier in this Preface).

We should like to thank the National Institute, not only for the excellent research facilities and stimulating atmosphere provided, but also for the opportunity to work together on such an enjoyable collaborative transatlantic project. Amongst the many individuals within the Institute, to whom we owe thanks for help in different ways at different times, we must mention in particular Andrew Britton, David Hitchens, Kit Jones, Fran Robinson and David Worswick. Very special thanks are due to Sig Prais. He has been closely involved with our work throughout its duration, offering countless thoughtful suggestions and insights on both content and presentation. We should also like to acknowledge the helpful comments of an anonymous referee. Needless to say, all remaining shortcomings in the book are our own responsibility.

Finally, the study forms part of the National Institute's programme of research on comparative industrial structure and efficiency sponsored by the Economic and Social Research Council and we should like to thank the Council for their financial support.

SWD
REC

ABBREVIATIONS

The following is a list of abbreviated definitions of all variables used in the econometric equations throughout the book. Appendix B provides more detailed definitions.

All variables are measured in comparative UK/US terms unless K or S is added at the end of the variable name (indicating British and American *levels* respectively). The addition of G at the end of a name indicates growth in the variable 1968–77.

AD	Advertising–sales ratio (*ADC* is the same, but for consumer convenience-goods industries only)
BEL	Index of disharmony in labour relations
CAP	Capital intensity (*CHECAP*, *BMCAP*, *ELCAP* denote capital intensity for industries within the Chemicals, Building Materials, Electrical and Instrument Engineering sectors)
COMP	Trade adjusted concentration ratio
C_5	5-firm concentration ratio
EFF	Labour productivity adjusted for capital intensity and plant size
ED	Average years of schooling of labour force
FOS	Incidence of foreign owned firms
IMEX	Sum of imports (*IM*) and exports (*EX*) deflated by market size
KBARR	Capital stock of typical size plant
MGR	Managerial input ⎫
NOPS	Non-operative input ⎬ All as proportions of the labour
PART	Part-time workers input ⎭ force
PCF	Female input
PRICE	Ratio of UK/US prices
TP	Typical plant size (*ELTP* denotes plant size in the Electrical and Instrument Engineering sector)
UNION	Proportionate trade union membership
VI	Index of vertical integration
RD	Research intensity (*MGRRDK* is *RDK* multiplied by *MGR*)
SIZE	Size of industry
SMAL	Incidence of small plants

STCOV	Proportion of workers directly involved in average strike
STRIK	Strikes per plant
PROFIT	Labour share in value-added
RAW	Proportion of industry's inputs from primary sectors
REGS	Index of regionality of United States industry
VPW	Labour productivity
VPW$_1$	Labour productivity for relatively larger plants
VPW$_2$	Labour productivity for relatively smaller plants
WAGE	Average wage per employee
WDL	Proportion of working days *not* lost through strikes

PRODUCTIVITY LEVELS IN BRITISH AND AMERICAN INDUSTRIES

Since World War II Britain has suffered a prolonged slide in its rank among industrial countries by level of real income per head. This decline has been a suspected cause of many other ills, such as inflationary pressures for higher money incomes and the political anguish of settling for a peripheral role in international affairs. The slow growth in income per head is closely allied to a slow expansion of productivity; indeed, one can so define 'productivity' to make it equivalent to income per head. Hypotheses abound concerning the causes of Britain's difficulties, with the culprits ranging from microeconomic malfunctions through inappropriate public policies to fundamental traits of culture and society. 'If Britain were different in respect of X, would productivity grow faster?' Orderly tests of these hypotheses have been few and largely confined to international comparisons of one feature at a time. Can the main trouble be strikes if the United States records more? Can Britain's leading companies be too small to compete internationally if Sweden's are smaller? And so on.

This paper extends previous research (Caves, 1980) that employed a new approach to testing the explanations of Britain's low or slow-growing productivity. We measure how much the productivity levels of British manufacturing industries differ from those in another major industrial country, the United States, and seek to explain why the productivity shortfall varies from one British industry to the next. This approach is of no help in evaluating forces that affect all British industries alike, such as broad features of the tax laws. But since many alleged causes of poor productivity performance should predictably weigh more heavily on some industries than on others, we seek to measure those factors and test their effects on productivity at the level of the individual manufacturing industry.

In this chapter we review the previous evidence on the causes of the shortfall in British industrial productivity. In Chapter 2 we present our own approach for analysing differences in the productivity of matched British and American manufacturing industries within a consistent framework based on the production function. Then in Chapter 3 we propose empirical embodiments for the hypotheses about the factors determining inter-industry variations in relative productivity and test them statistically for the years 1967/8 and 1977. The next three chapters offer extensions of this approach. In Chapter 4 we extend the results of

Chapter 3 into a simultaneous-equations framework, on the expectation that productivity, relative prices, total production, and flows of exports and imports are determined jointly. In Chapter 5 we disaggregate the matched UK/US industries into their large-plant and small-plant components, to explore the degree to which productivity problems repose in a conjunction of managerial deficiencies and combative labour relations in large plants. In Chapter 6 we apply this inter-industry approach to productivity growth over the period 1968–77, to determine whether the factors depressing industries' productivity levels similarly affect their rates of productivity growth. Chapter 7 closes the study with a consideration of its policy implications.

THE STATISTICAL RECORD

The negative evidence on British productivity has been appearing so regularly that news of fresh disasters has lost most of its capacity to shock. Nonetheless, we report some central findings in order to indicate the dimensions of the phenomenon. A useful perspective is provided by a recently published study of total factor productivity and its components in the United Kingdom and eight other countries (Christensen, Cummings and Jorgenson, 1981); although it only brings the evidence to 1973, it does cover two decades of the period since World War II. Its principal results are summarised in table 1.1. Britain's output per head in 1970[1] was 54.6 per cent of that of the United States, ahead of Italy but behind Japan and the major European countries. Total factor productivity was better, 74.2 per cent of that in the United States, but still lower than for the other countries (including Italy). Britain's capital input per head was greater than that of Italy and Japan but less than that of the other European countries. Its labour input per head was in the middle of the European distribution although much below Japan's. That labour input can be disaggregated into the three components: employment per head, hours worked per employee, and education per employee. Britain's position on the former two is normal, but its education input seems low.[2] Thus, these data mark Britain's inputs of physical and human capital and its residual productivity as potential bases for explaining the productivity shortfall.

Table 1.1 also contains data on total factor productivity for 1955. In that year British total factor productivity was only 66.8 per cent of that in the United States. Thus, whatever the deficiencies of productivity growth in Britain, it exceeded total factor productivity growth in the United States during the period 1955–73, although the other countries covered in the study gained on the United States even more rapidly. Interestingly, the data of Christensen, Cummings, and Jorgenson (1981) indicate that most of the catch-up with United States total factor productivity took place in the

Table 1.1. *Total factor productivity and its components, United Kingdom, France, Germany, and Japan relative to the United States*

Productivity element	Year	UK	France	Germany	Japan
Total factor productivity	1970	0.742	0.788	0.909	0.799
Output per head	1970	0.546	0.657	0.721	0.583
Capital input per head	1970	0.540	0.702	0.709	0.325
Labour input per head	1970	0.907	0.966	0.850	1.346
Employment per head	1970	1.105	1.069	1.152	1.226
Hours worked	1970	1.090	1.114	1.112	1.201
Education	1970	0.753	0.811	0.663	0.915
Total factor productivity	1955	0.668	0.567	0.609	0.482

Sources: Christensen, Cummings and Jorgenson (1981), tables 1, 2, 7.

period 1968–73, when all of the countries they studied reduced their shortfalls by 5 to 10 per cent.[3] Over a longer period of time, data on output per head indicate a similar pattern of slow growth. Maddison's (1977) data suggest a fourfold growth in output per head for the United Kingdom over 1870–1976; fifteen other industrial countries averaged nearly an eightfold increase, and only one grew more slowly. Germany's GDP per head, 36 per cent lower than Britain's at the turn of the century, had become 29 per cent higher by 1973, and Italy's climbed to equality with Britain's from a level 63 per cent lower.

The data summarised in table 1.1 agree with a substantial amount of information on comparative labour productivity that has become available in recent years. Jones (1976) compared the United Kingdom and the original members of the European Community in the growth of gross value-added per man-hour in manufacturing. He found that France and Germany attained higher labour productivity in 1955, and Italy's level reached that of Britain in 1968. Smith, Hitchens, and Davies (1982) used data normalised for international price differentials for Britain, Germany, and the United States to estimate relative labour productivity in six broad sectors. As of 1977 labour productivity in British manufacturing was only 66 per cent of that in Germany and 34 per cent of that in the United States. Britain's relative performance in all industrial sectors, taken together, was actually somewhat better than in manufacturing: 70 and 38 per cent respectively (see table 1.2). Roy (1982) brought the comparison of aggregate and sectoral output per employed worker up to 1980, placing Britain's output per employed worker in manufacturing at only 49 per cent of Germany's (but up to 40 per cent of the United States). Roy's corresponding figures for overall GDP at market prices are 68 per cent and 60 per cent respectively, implying a substantial catch-up with the United

Table 1.2. *Comparative labour productivity, United Kingdom, Germany, and United States, selected sectors, 1968 and 1977*

Year	Agriculture	Extractive industries	Manu- facturing	Con- struction	Public utilities	All industry
UK/US						
1968	0.41	0.15	0.35	0.49	0.23	0.36
1977	0.48	0.29	0.34	0.59	0.33	0.38
UK/Germany						
1968	1.30	0.50	0.74	0.58	0.57	0.79
1977	1.22	0.66	0.66	0.46	0.55	0.70

Source: Calculated from Smith, Hitchens, and Davies (1982, p. 5).

States and growth equal to Germany's during the 1970s. Thus, the recent evidence tends to place Britain still behind in the race but possibly gaining on the leaders, and the rapid growth of productivity in manufacturing during the first half of the 1980s sustains this unaccustomed tinge of optimism.[4]

Studies of productivity in sectors other than manufacturing have given generally similar results. Smith and Hitchens (1983) found that labour productivity in Britain's retail distribution sector was 45.5 per cent of that in the United States, and that the shortfall could not be accounted for by differences in services provided or in sectoral composition. Nor are differences in the prevalence of multi-unit retailers an adequate explanation.

Because our research design emphasises the competitive testing of hypotheses about the comparative efficiency of British manufacturing industries, we now survey the evidence that has accumulated on three principal alleged problem areas: labour relations, quality of managerial and other human capital, and sizes of plants and companies. Although these areas will turn out to have an important confluence, it is convenient to consider the evidence on them separately.

LABOUR RELATIONS

Britain's system of labour relations in the workplace, rooted ultimately in class and social attitudes, has been argued to impair industrial productivity in a number of ways.[5] The system both reflects and reinforces the preference of workers for a secure job and restrictive work rules, at the expense of higher wages. The preference for restrictive practices in turn makes adequate quality control more costly and delays the introduction of technological change. The lack of a binding legal framework deprives managements of contractual assurance about the short-run continuity of their labour supply and therefore about the levels of output they can achieve. Quantitative evidence has gradually accumulated to shed light on the paths by which productivity is affected by the system of labour relations. These include strikes, restrictive work rules, policy overtime, and the cost to management of dealing with labour-relations problems.

Strikes

The loss of production through strikes is one element of industrial relations that does not indict the system of labour relations, despite some deterioration in the 1970s. Data covering the period since World War II fail to put Britain very high among industrial countries in the number of working days recorded as lost due to strikes per 1,000 employees. Britain's relative performance also improves if the comparison is confined to countries with relatively similar systems of industrial relations, such as the United States and Canada. But Smith (1980) found that during the 1970s Britain's rank among countries in the working days lost due to strikes deteriorated faster than the rank of any other major industrial country. That may have reflected not worsening structural conditions but rather uncertainty about the country's high inflation rate, which has been found to provoke additional strike activity (Turk, 1984).

The incidence of strikes is usually expected to increase with the size of plant. In large plants relations between workers and management are less personal than in small plants and thus more disputes occur. There are also more interactions among work groups in large plants and therefore more bases for stoppages over jurisdictional issues, work rules, and the like. Prais (1981, Chapter 7) developed a model of large plants' greater potential for disputes by positing that each plant contains a number of work groups, the number increasing with the plant's size. He also assumed a fixed probability that any one group will get into a dispute (with management or with another employee group) during a given period. This model, he found, predicts quite well the actual increase in the number of disputes with the size of British plants. The relation between plant size and disputes should not be peculiar to Britain, of course, but Prais showed empirically that it operates more strongly in Britain than in either Germany or the United States. He found that two-thirds of the difference in strike-proneness among the seventeen principal divisions of the United Kingdom manufacturing sector can be explained by differences in their distributions of plant sizes. Marginson (1984) used data on a large panel of plants to show that the occurrence of strikes is related to size of the plant and not to the size of the company operating it. Thus, the problem is associated with the workplace and not with the administrative organisation that controls it.

Restrictive rules

A second quantifiable effect of the industrial relations system is low productivity on the job because of work rules, overmanning, resistance to innovation, and the like. A number of investigations, both official and private, have looked into the sources of poor productivity in certain major 'problem' industries: shipbuilding, chemicals, printing, motor vehicles, mechanical engineering, and textiles. For all sectors but textiles the reports regularly mention constraints on productivity due to such restrictive labour practices as demarcation rules (between crafts) and union rules involving the use of assistants. Union structure is also mentioned as a problem for these sectors, as are strikes for shipbuilding and motor vehicles.[6] It may be that for structural reasons these are problem industries in other countries as well. Hence, studies that have made international comparisons of productivity differences provide a valuable check. They frequently report outright overmanning, possibly a failure of management, although that seems unlikely when the comparison involves multinational companies, which should be able to apply the best available management practices in Britain. The fact that overmanning often occurs in auxiliary functions (maintenance, canteen services, and so on), where craft unions are important, seems to signify restrictive labour practices. Comparative studies suggest that demarcation rules increase the time required to repair breakdowns of equipment, exacting manifest costs in productivity. Furthermore, evidence is accumulating that overmanning is partly a response to the problem of maintaining product quality.[7]

Pratten (1976, p. 61), reviewing productivity comparisons that multinational companies have made among their international plants, hazarded a guess about the maximum proportion of the productivity differences between Britain and other countries that could be attributed to labour relations. This maximum is roughly one-fourth of the United Kingdom's productivity shortfall relative to Canada and the United States, one-third of that relative to France, and one-half of that relative to Germany.

Policy overtime

A third quantifiable effect of labour relations on productivity is the persistence of policy overtime: long work-weeks demanded by low-wage workers to fatten their thin pay packets. Overtime would have no adverse effect on productivity, properly measured, if it were undertaken sporadically to meet temporary or unexpected increases in demand. But it can become a drag on productivity if it is built into the labour bargain *and* results in no net increase in output (or not enough to offset the marginal disutility of extra hours spent on the job). Because overtime evidently fluctuates in response to aggregate demand, it is not caused solely by a degenerate wage bargain. Nevertheless, the number of overtime hours worked shows a significant negative relation to average hourly earnings in the United Kingdom but not in the United States, a strong indication that overtime serves to fill out the weekly pay (Leslie, 1976).

The National Board for Prices and Incomes (1970, pp. 51, 104, 105) found substantial shop-floor pressure to maintain overtime hours. The board's questionnaire study did not mark trade unions as pressing for overtime, but it did show that managers use overtime more frequently to meet normal demand than to meet peaks, and that a large minority of manual workers expect it regularly. The report also found that plants reporting extensive overtime tended to show manifest opportunities to improve efficiency, and one-third of the employers surveyed concurred that the productivity of most workers during *regular* hours is at least occasionally affected adversely by the presence of overtime opportunities (National Board for Prices and Incomes, 1970, pp. 52, 106, 107).

Other resource costs

Productivity shortfall also results from the excess costs incurred by managements in dealing with labour relations. These take the forms of either outright drains on resources or decreases in the effectiveness of the company caused by increased uncertainty about the rate of output. Numerous types of such losses have been identified:

Firstly, because of strikes and disruptions at supplier companies, managers find it necessary to hold larger inventories of raw materials and goods in process than managements of comparable firms in other countries. The Central Policy Review Staff (1975, pp. 26, 75) noted that one continental vehicle plant dependent on British supplies held a twenty-day inventory, whereas a comparable Japanese plant might hold a few hours' worth. Similar evidence has appeared for other industries.[8]

Secondly, uncertainties about output rates leave companies unsure about how much output will be available for sale, thereby reducing the effectiveness of the resources allocated to marketing activity. In continental plants making automobile components, monthly production rates seldom vary from planned output by more than 5 per cent, whereas variances of 20 per cent or more are common in British plants. Companies' cash flows are destabilised, and distribution channels become periodically under-utilised, or buyers discount their willingness to pay for the product because of the uncertainty of delivery.[9]

Thirdly, companies bringing new equipment on stream face demands that the resulting productivity gains be shared with the workforce. The dilution of the cost savings and reduction in the rate of return on the investment, when these demands are successful, may be less costly than the uncertainty about how long disputes over manning will keep newly installed equipment idle. A metal container company reported that a new line producing two-piece cans was running at 40 to 50 per cent of capacity, largely because of difficulties in labour relations (Price Commission, 1978, pp. 7, 24; Pratten, 1976, pp. 55–6; Prais, 1981, pp. 254–5).

Fourthly, the marked tendency for labour relations to deteriorate as plant size increases may encourage British companies to build plants smaller than would otherwise be indicated by technical economies of scale, and interviews with executives have confirmed that plants become unmanageable as the number of employees grows much beyond 500 (Caves, 1980, p. 147). The use of specialised personnel dealing with labour relations correspondingly increases with plant size (Marginson, 1984), although we do not know whether the increase is more pronounced than in other countries.

Finally, management time is diverted to problems of labour relations and away from other tasks. Plant managers in the British car industry claim to spend almost half of their time dealing with labour disputes, their counterparts in Belgium and Germany only 5 to 10 per cent (Central Policy Review Staff, 1975, p. 99). The fact that British managers must be more in evidence on the plant floor, to deal with the problems that arise, is itself a source of friction (Pratten, 1976, p. 56). Perhaps more insidious, the uncertainty of labour relations affects the criteria for evaluating the plant manager's performance, marking for success the resourceful improviser who can scramble to keep things moving on a day-to-day basis. This priority is likely to prove hostile to effective long-range planning at the top.

SKILLS OF MANAGEMENT AND LABOUR

A second group of explanations offered for the shortfall of productivity lies in under-investment in human capital. This hypothesis is applied both to the workforce in general and to managers in particular. In this guise it shades into the hypothesis that the quality of management is deficient. We consider the two together, noting that poor managerial performance could result either from inadequate human capital investment or from cultural and social characteristics that impair the performance of the managerial function. In this latter guise the hypothesis is somewhat unsatisfying, because in its usual formulation it leaves the entrepreneur to carry the residual burden of opprobrium for low productivity after everyone else has either been absolved or stuck with some share of the responsibility. Productivity could be low either because management really is ineffective, or because management cannot triumph over hostile forces that have gone unmeasured by the investigator. We therefore concentrate on specific evidence capable of laying blame for low productivity at the door of the executive suite (or removing it therefrom).

The principal controlled-experiment evidence on managerial effectiveness — now rather dated — comes from Dunning's studies of the comparative performance of British companies and competing foreign enterprises, both in Britain and in Canada and the United States. Dunning's (1970, Chapter 9) analysis of data for the years around 1960 showed that 51 of 80 American subsidiary companies attained higher productivity than their United Kingdom competitors and earned correspondingly higher average profits. The comparison could be biased, however, because of our Darwinian expectation that multinational companies embody (or embodied) a higher level of competence than run-of-the-mill firms, or they would not have become multinational. Yet there is also evidence that subsidiaries of British companies operating in North America did less well on average than their local competitors; even joint ventures with local companies were on average slightly more profitable than fully owned subsidiaries (Dunning, 1970, Chapter 6). This result still does not clinch the case against British management, because the lower profits of British subsidiaries in North America might, as Dunning pointed out, be due to their tenancy in slower-growing and less profitable industries.

Later evidence supports these findings, although only in part. Dunning and Pearce (1977, pp. 69–70) found that companies affiliated with American parents remain more profitable than the British companies that are their direct competitors, and the United States affiliates continue to use younger and more highly qualified executives. American affiliates, however, are not concentrated in the most profitable industries; their average profit rate on sales would actually increase by 7 per cent if they were distributed among industries in the same way as all British quoted companies. Moreover their overall profit rate on total capital was falling relative to that of leading British companies: 92 per cent higher in 1950–4 but only 20 per cent higher in 1970–3.[10] The results of Solomon and Ingham (1977) cast doubt on whether foreign subsidiaries attain higher productivity than domestic firms in the mechanical engineering sector. We cannot rule out the hypothesis that foreign entrepreneurs are generally at a disadvantage in extracting physical productivity on (what is for them) foreign soil, but accept the situation because of offsetting advantages that they command in non-production activities.

This last possibility is underlined by the evidence that multinational enterprises have not outperformed their British competitors in managing their labour relations. Although Steuer and Gennard (1971) found that the multinationals attained lower strike frequencies, Forsyth (1973) concluded (from Scottish data) that they do worse, and Creigh and Makeham (1978) found no difference after controlling the industry's labour intensity and the sizes of its plants. Overall, the evidence from comparisons between foreign affiliates and domestic companies still seems to support the hypothesis of inferior British management performance, but not conclusively.

Investment in human resources

However one reads the evidence on the performance of British management, it seems clear that low investments in managerial training are a possible explanation for underperformance. Crockett and Elias (1984) used data from the National Training Survey to show that managers hold only marginally more qualifications than the population at large. Younger managers have more, but 'there is little evidence of an increase in the proportion of younger managers who hold qualifications which are directly related to a managerial education.' A substantial proportion of managers have worked their way up from semi-skilled first jobs; Crockett and Elias also found that managers' earnings are not especially sensitive to training and education variables, although they show significant differences based on categories of managerial functions (with personal and experience attributes controlled). Thus, if we accept the hypothesis that managerial performance explains some of the problems of productivity levels, under-investment and under-valuation of managerial skills should take some of the blame.[11]

That brings the issue back to the general level of skills and training. The possibility that low investment in skills accounts for low labour productivity has, of course, an impeccable neoclassical foundation. However, the available evidence indicates that low skill levels may have some subtle but important consequences for the organisation of production and the quality of output.

Although economists have often measured national differences in educational investment simply by years of schooling, recent investigation of the qualitative characteristics of British vocational training have shown that under-investment can take more subtle forms. Prais and Wagner (1983), comparing the training systems in five occupations, contrasted Germany's practice of testing acquired skills under examination conditions with the British orientation towards serving time as an apprentice. Daly, Hitchens, and Wagner (1985) associated skill differences between workforces in matched British and German plants with the Germans' ability to deliver more complex or higher quality products (also Prais, 1981, pp. 130, 179–86). Skill differences also proved relevant to the German plants' ability to utilise more sophisticated equipment and to repair it promptly following breakdowns. Thus, it seems probable that Britain suffers from the low intensity of the vocational training that is provided, and from the cumulation of low skill levels from operatives through to managers that limits the ability of British plants to employ sophisticated equipment and processes and to turn out complex products. Notice that 'managerial failure' in this guise runs through the whole supervisory hierarchy and does not occur only in the directors' offices.

An implication of this hypothesis is that the remedy involves not just an increase in the level of investment in human capital but a close look at the qualitative characteristics of the training that is provided. Daly (1982) reported the similarity among the United States, Britain, and Germany in their populations' average amounts of full-time schooling as well as the evidence of declining returns to education in all of them during the 1970s. She voiced scepticism of the conclusions from macroeconomic studies of output and productivity that increased investment in education automatically yields substantial real returns.

Some aggregative evidence on Britain's effective position in workforce skills comes from studies of the pattern of international trade. Katrak (1973) reached the conclusion that Britain specialises in manufactures that embody lower skills and accordingly sell at lower unit prices than those of the United States.[12] At least in mechanical engineering exports, this pattern grew more evident over the period 1962–76 (Connell, 1979). Katrak later (1982) investigated the skill intensity of United Kingdom exports relative to that of goods competing with British imports. He found that exports continue to embody more skills and more research inputs than import replacements, but that the margin seems to have declined over the decade 1968–78. A similar conclusion flows from the data on Britain's earnings from foreign investment and her payments to direct investors based in other countries.

SIZES OF COMPANIES AND PLANTS

Another factor related to industrial efficiency is the sizes of plants and companies, and the industry-specific character of this determinant of performance makes it natural to emphasise in this investigation. In the 1960s Britain went through a period of romance with corporate bigness. Size, efficiency, and advanced technology were declared inseparable; policy was based on the belief that merging the leading companies in British industries would somehow both increase their efficiency and improve their ability to stand up to foreign rivals.[13] Abundant research testifies to the existence of technical economies of scale that may be quite important in some industries. Whether British plants and companies have under-exploited them, however, is not clear. Although scale economies have lost much of their fascination for policy-makers, their possible role in explaining Britain's productivity has not been resolved.

Sizes of companies

A good deal of information has accumulated on the comparative sizes of plants and companies in the United Kingdom and other countries in the European Community. Because of a pervasive relation between the sizes of

European Community. Because of a pervasive relation between the sizes of plants and companies and the sizes of their national markets, British firms are more aptly compared to those in similar-size continental countries than to those in the United States. George and Ward (1975, Chapter 3), who analysed the four leading firms in 41 industries, found the British companies to be larger on average than their German counterparts in 29 of these industries, larger than French firms in 37 industries, and larger than Italian ones in 40. They attributed the differences to laws that have discouraged collusion but permitted mergers in the United Kingdom, whereas the continental countries have been more tolerant of collusion and of the coordination of competing firms through banking connections. Seller concentration is correspondingly higher in Britain: the four largest companies accounted for a weighted average share of 30 per cent of shipments in Britain, 22 per cent in France, and 19 per cent in Germany and Italy (George and Ward, 1975, p. 17).

Moreover, Britain invariably outscores Germany when the largest European firms, not only the leading ones in individual industries, are taken into consideration. In *Fortune*'s list of the largest 500 companies outside the United States for 1984, Britain accounted for 88, following Japan (136) but ahead of Germany (58) and France (38).[14] *Fortune*'s list undesirably includes overseas subsidiaries of United States companies; a more careful tabulation by Herman Daems (1985, table 1) of independent European organisational hierarchies employing 10,000 or more assigns no less than 119 of 313 (38 per cent) to Britain, followed by Germany with 57 (18 per cent) and France with 43 (14 per cent).

Whatever these standings, within Britain there has evidently been a weak tendency over the years 1960–76 for the smaller of the 2,000 largest companies to grow faster than the larger ones, while before that period a similarly weak tendency ran in the opposite direction (Kumar, 1985). Similarly, Britain's share of Europe's largest companies has been eroding somewhat; for this the country's slower growth is a likely explanation. Britain's largest firms are concentrated in food and drink, tobacco, textiles, paper, and building materials, while Germany's cluster in electrical engineering, chemicals, metals and metal products, but with this difference noted one surely cannot conclude that British companies are in general too small to stand up to their European rivals.[15] If British firms were too small, we should expect the combination of independent companies into larger business units to generate some measurable economic successes. The evidence points, in fact, in just the opposite direction. Whether the eye falls upon large-scale combinations promoted by public policy or the outcomes of ordinary commercial mergers and acquisitions, success has on average neither been anticipated by the securities market (at the time of the event) nor realised subsequently.[16]

Sizes of plants

That British firms' sizes at least match those in the European countries suggests, but does not prove, that plant sizes are also comparable. Indeed, in some important industries such as steel, British plants do appear to be both smaller and older than those on the continent (Cockerill, 1974; Aylen, 1982). Comparisons based on employment size do not show any pervasive difference, although we must remember that a British plant matching its European rivals in employment size will typically be smaller if the comparison is based on output. In the typical industry, the size of the median plant tends to increase with the size of the national market in which it operates (Pryor, 1972), and so comparisons with the continental countries remain the appropriate ones. Thus, George and Ward (1975, pp. 29–30) found that the 20 largest plants in each of 47 manufacturing industries were about the same size in Britain and Germany. The average size (weighted by industry employment) was 3,730 employees in Germany, 3,130 in Britain, 2,090 in France, and 990 in Italy. In terms of employment, the leading German plants were larger than the leading British ones in 24 of the 47 industries. Prais (1981, Chapters 2 and 3) found British median plant sizes (again measured by employment) similar to those in Germany, while exceeding them in the upper quartile of the distribution and in fact matching the United States upper quartile. Subdivided by industry, German plants seem larger in the 'heavy' industries where plant economies of scale are expected to obtain, such as motor vehicles, ferrous metals, chemicals, machine tools, and office machinery. In light industries, British median and upper-quartile plant sizes tend to exceed the United States and Germany.

Hughes (1976, pp. 88–91) noted that in Germany manufacturing became increasingly concentrated in large plants over 1958–68, while British manufacturing remained relatively unchanged. This difference could have resulted from either differences in the overall rates of economic growth in the two countries or factors that inhibited the organisation of work in large plants in Britain (such as the problems of labour relations, discussed above). Even so, large plants remain abundant in the United Kingdom, and the proportion of small manufacturing plants is lower than in any other industrial country. The Bolton committee, using 200 employees as the cut-off for small establishments, found that in the 1960s 31 per cent of manufacturing employment was in small establishments, compared with 34 per cent in Germany, 39 per cent in the United States, 47 per cent in Canada, and 53 per cent in Sweden.[17]

The facts regarding comparative plant sizes are clearer than their normative interpretation. On the one hand, the enlargement of market opportunities through the proportional expansion of international trade in general (and market enlargement in the European Community, in particular) has evidently provided substantial opportunities for productivity gains through larger and more specialised production facilities (Owen, 1983; Harris, 1984). On the other, the interaction between plant size and divisive labour relations in Britain raises the threat that the United Kingdom may be poorly positioned to obtain such gains, at least in industries that suffer the most from labour-relations problems. It is no surprise that the case studies undertaken by Prais (1981) show no evident association between plant sizes and productivity in British industries relative to their American and German counterparts.

Concentration of producers

Against this background we can usefully place the evidence on the changing concentration of producers in British manufacturing. As Hart and Clarke (1980) showed, concentration in United Kingdom manufacturing industries has been increasing much more rapidly than in their American counterparts, with the British increase especially swift during 1958–68. Because this increase can hardly have served to repair suboptimal plant and/or firm sizes, on the evidence just cited, one wonders what relation it does bear to the efficiency of British manufacturing. Hart and Clarke's findings associate the increase much more with increasing plants per firm than with increasing plant sizes. Similarly, while the extent of mergers' contribution to the increase has been controversial, it was large on any reckoning.[18] Finally, whatever caused the increase, it was not the changing economies of large-scale sales promotion, which propelled the increase in the United States. Therefore, one may doubt that changes in the industrial structure of British manufacturing have played any productivity-increasing role, whatever their ultimate causes may have been.

PRODUCTIVITY CONSTRAINTS AND THEIR SOCIAL CONTEXT

The principal hypotheses about low productivity, reviewed above, have a conspicuous intersection. Low productivity is alleged to stem from a divisive and balkanised organisation of the labour force and management deficient in skill or training. Both shortcomings are evidently at their worst in large plants and industries that require large-scale and complex organisation for economic success. These hypotheses evidently satisfy the requisites of our research design. They vary from sector to sector, holding out the possibility of statistical inference based on inter-industry differences in relative productivity.

If these hypotheses are correct, we should expect to find casual confirmation in the sectoral organisation of the economy and its rewards to factors of production. Such evidence falls readily to hand. Ray (1984b) showed that total hourly labour costs (including social charges) were lower in Britain than in fourteen other countries, with Japan being higher by 4 per cent, Finland and France by 15 per cent, and Austria and the Netherlands by 18 per cent. Low productivity means low real wages and limited incentives to substitute other inputs for labour or seek ways to improve its productivity,

Similarly, if British productivity is relatively low in industries whose technologies call for large-scale but labour-intensive production and/or sophisticated management, we should expect these industries to prove weak competitors for the country's stock of factors of production, as comparative-advantage adjustments propel that stock toward less disadvantaged sectors (capital-intensive or process-technology industries, sectors with small minimum efficient scales of production or limited requirements for sophisticated managerial systems). Ray (1984a) found evidence consistent with the predicted structural shifts in the economy as some industries were competed down by imports or enlarged by fast-growing demand, while the positions of others depended on the effects of relative price changes interacting with market demands that might or might not be elastic. Williams, Williams, and Thomas (1983) argued that the share of manufactures in British imports, advancing much more rapidly than their share in exports, was another consequence of manufacturing's ineffective use of resources.[19]

A major question about these principal hypotheses is their potential relevance to public policy. If the causes of low productivity are rooted deep in the nation's social structure, the conventional instruments of public policy may be unable to offer substantial remedies. Indeed, the institutional depth of these forces is readily apparent. For example, Phelps Brown (1977) invoked history to explain the apparent preference of trade unions for restrictive arrangements. Union members never experienced a revolution, a defeat in war, or a foreign occupation to dislodge them from ancient values and attitudes. Because, unlike their American counterparts, British trade unions never knew a period when jobs were plentiful, the need for 'keeping a place' was instilled in their members at the start. In the twentieth century the closing down of some of the oldest industries (coal mines, textiles) 'may well have had its effect on the outlook of more than those who lost their jobs . . . It seems that the concentration of hardship, the frustrated lives and stricken communities, made a greater impact than the diffusion of new employment that was in fact going on' (pp. 20-2).

But trade unions are only part of the fabric of British institutions, a fabric with a matchless record of continuity and accommodation. The survival of that fabric, untattered by invasion or revolution, has provided interest groups with legitimacy to defend and preserve a wide range of interests in the political arena. As Olson (1982) stressed, the goals that these groups pursue are collective goods for their members. Because of the free-rider problem, such groups are formed only with difficulty and emerge only in a stable and tolerant environment. Once in place they are at their most effective in blocking changes that will affect them adversely. The average citizen stands to gain from the economy's efficient adaptation to change and innovation, whereas special-interest groups hold much more concentrated interests in forestalling changes that threaten their quasi-rents. Rather than holding out for lump-sum compensation as the price for being on the losing end of a socially desirable change, interest groups find both their self-esteem and their committed personal assets better served by blocking the change itself. Although this process is most easily seen in politics, it also affects the pursuit of economic efficiency. Efficiency is to an important degree the ability to make optimal adaptations to changes in one's circumstances. An encrusted institutional structure is therefore likely to delay change and thus reduce the growth rate of productivity, as well as to frustrate the search for the more efficient and productive arrangements attainable in any given set of circumstances.

Whatever may be the scope for change, it is important to know what most needs changing. Economic analyses of Britain's problems have pointed, with evidence, to a host of factors, all of which may be relevant in varying degrees in different industries. The task of the present study is to carry out an analysis for a broad range of manufacturing industries, in order to confirm and evaluate the relative contributions of the major factors involved.

2

RELATIVE INDUSTRIAL PRODUCTIVITY: AN ANALYTICAL FRAMEWORK

Many if not all of the principal hypotheses about lagging British productivity should affect various manufacturing industries differently. That is the basis of our research design, which involves matching as many United Kingdom manufacturing industries as possible to their United States counterparts, calculating the ratio of net output per head (value-added per worker, in American parlance) in the British industry to that in its American counterpart, and explaining the inter-industry variance in the resulting labour productivity ratios. In this chapter we develop the theoretical basis for this research design.

The analysis of productivity differentials industry by industry is not a new idea, and can be traced back to Rostas (1948), Frankel (1957), Paige and Bombach (1959), West (1971), Chandrasekar (1973), and Yukizawa (1975). These studies, however, were concerned mainly with describing the magnitudes of international differences in productivity, and sought to explain them (if at all) only by a sketchy selection of causal factors. Researchers interested in the industrial efficiency of Canada and Australia have developed the research design more fully, but with reference to a set of hypotheses quite different from the ones applicable to Britain.[1]

THE CORE NEOCLASSICAL MODEL

Productivity is fundamentally a relationship between the value of an industry's output and the inputs that give rise to it. Labour productivity, which is our dependent variable, is only an approximation to it. We need to incorporate into the determinants of relative labour productivity the other principal inputs (physical and human capital) as well as the factor of economies of scale. Suppose that the production function of the ith plant in a given industry takes the familiar Cobb-Douglas form:

$$Y_i = A K_i^{\alpha} L_i^{\beta} \qquad i = 1, \ldots, N \tag{1}$$

Here Y stands for net output, K for capital input, and L for labour input. A is the efficiency parameter, and the sum of the coefficients $\alpha + \beta$ indicates the extent of returns to scale. We want to aggregate this function over the N plants in the industry and express it with Y/L as the left-hand-side variable, in line with the empirical procedure proposed above. We first simplify the aggregation problem by assuming that each plant has not only the same production function but also is the same size, so that its inputs are equal to the average inputs of all plants in the industry: $L_i = \bar{L}$; $K_i = \bar{K}$. Then we can write the following expression for the industry's labour productivity:

$$\frac{Y}{L} = \frac{NA\bar{K}^\alpha \bar{L}^\beta}{NL} = A\left(\frac{K}{L}\right)^\alpha \bar{L}^{\alpha+\beta-1} \tag{2}$$

where Y, K, and L denote industry aggregates. Thus, the Cobb-Douglas form implies that labour productivity will equal the product of the efficiency parameter, the capital–labour ratio, and the average size of plant.

Because plant sizes are diverse in the typical industry, we need to allow for the N plants differing in size. We do assume, however, that all employ the same capital intensity: $K_i/L_i = K/L$ (but see note 2 below). Substitute this weaker assumption into (1), summing over the N plants and dividing by L, and the industry's labour productivity can now be written:

$$\frac{Y}{L} = A\left(\left(\frac{K}{L}\right)^\alpha \left[L^{\alpha+\beta-1} \sum \left(\frac{L_i}{L}\right)^{\alpha+\beta}\right]\right) \tag{3}$$

We now introduce the following definition:

$$P = L\left[\sum \left(\frac{L_i}{L}\right)^{\alpha+\beta}\right]^{\frac{1}{\alpha+\beta-1}} \tag{4}$$

which enables us to rewrite (3) as

$$\frac{Y}{L} = A\left(\frac{K}{L}\right)^\alpha P^{\alpha+\beta-1} \tag{5}$$

Comparison of (5) with (2) reveals that the only difference is the replacement of $\bar{L}$ by P. Because we shall argue below that P is an alternative measure of typical plant size, better suited to the size distributions of plants found in the real world, we interpret (5) as confirming the relationship between productivity and capital intensity and typical plant size.

We can see the implications of this analysis for a regression model in which the dependent variable is relative labour productivity, hereafter *VPW*. Define the following variables for a given industry, with the subscripts K and S indicating United Kingdom and United States respectively:

$$CAP \equiv (K/L)_K / (K/L)_S$$
$$TP \equiv P_K / P_S$$
$$EFF \equiv A_K / A_S$$

Now make the assumption that the output-elasticity coefficients α and β are the same for all sampled industries in both countries. Then for any industry j we can write:

$$VPW_j = EFF_j * CAP_j^\alpha * TP_j^{\alpha+\beta-1} \qquad (6)$$

When we take logarithms and add a disturbance term, we have a linear stochastic relationship between comparative productivity and comparative efficiency, comparative capital-intensity, and comparative plant size that can serve as the basis for a regression analysis of VPW. The variables CAP and TP are observable, and the regression coefficients will provide estimated values for α and $(\alpha+\beta-1)$. EFF captures all influences on productivity other than quantities of capital and labour. Our hypotheses about the determinants of relative productivity then take the implicit form of a functional relationship determining EFF that can be substituted into equation (6).[2]

This procedure can be visualised with the aid of Chart 2.1, which presents the familiar isoquants that indicate quantities of (net) output obtained from various inputs of capital and labour. Let Y_K be the quantity of net output that a randomly selected British industry actually produces;

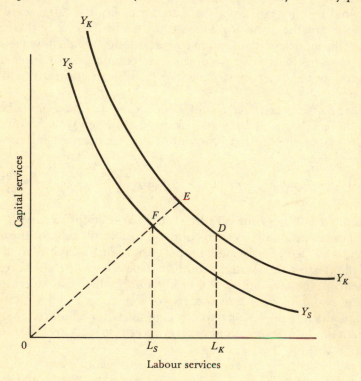

Chart 2.1 *A diagrammatic representation of* EFF

the isoquant with that label depicts all combinations of capital and labour from which it could be obtained. D indicates the combination actually employed, and L_K indicates the associated labour input. Our method implicitly identifies by point F the amount of labour that would be required to produce Y_K in the United States, where it would require labour input L_S. The isoquant Y_S is provisionally treated as drawn from the same production function as Y_K, but with a different level of efficiency. Point F's position on Y_S of course reflects the capital–labour proportions actually used in the United States. Equation (6) resolves the difference between points D and F into these components: by means of CAP it adjusts for the United Kingdom production point being at D rather than at E (United States factor proportions); by means of TP it repositions the United Kingdom isoquant to the one that would pertain with identical plant scales; it identifies OF/OE as the residual measure of efficiency EFF to be explained by qualitative differences in inputs and by all other factors that bear on pure differences in efficiency.

Differences in production functions

It is obviously undesirable to assume that the output-elasticities of capital and labour are the same for all sampled industries in both countries. Although the industry cross-section research design breaks down if we allow them to vary freely, we can accommodate certain generic inter-industry and inter-country differences. Specifically, we can address the following conditions:

1. *α and β differ between the United Kingdom and the United States but are the same for all industries in each country.* In this case, when we take the ratio of equation (5) for the United Kingdom to its counterpart for the United States, we obtain:

$$VPW_j = EFF_j * CAP_j^{\alpha_S} TP_j^{\alpha_S + \beta_S - 1} CAPK_j^{\alpha_K - \alpha_S} TPK_j^{\alpha_K + \beta_K - \alpha_S - \beta_S} \tag{7}$$

which should hold true for all observed pairs of industries, with α and β assumed the same for all j in each country. This result calls for the addition of two variables to our regression model (equation 6): capital intensity and typical plant size in the United Kingdom ($CAPK$ and TPK). The regression coefficients of these variables will hold considerable economic interest. If $CAPK_j$ is found to take a negative coefficient, it implies that capital systematically proves less productive in Britain. Similarly, a negative coefficient for TPK_j implies that greater returns to scale are obtained in the United States.[3]

2. *α and β in industry j are the same in both countries but differ between industries.* If these coefficients differ freely among industries, as one would generally assume, then the pure cross-section methodology that we employ breaks

down. However, casual inspection of the standard industrial classification suggests that industries are grouped therein according to general technological similarities that can be identified from their input combinations. Econometrically, we can take these differences among industry groups into account by including dummy slope variables for CAP and TP in each sector for which different values of α and β are expected to obtain. Once we have allowed for inter-sectoral differences in the impact of capital intensity and plant size, we shall suppose that the marginal effects of the determinants of EFF are the same for all industries. The process of filling out equation (7) with the variables thought to determine EFF is discussed below.

Measuring typical plant size

We suggested that P (defined in equation (4)) can be interpreted as a measure of typical plant size and that it is measurable empirically. These assertions rest on the theory of measurement of industrial concentration. The comparison of concentration of sellers in different markets is complicated by the fact that the industries concerned may have very different size distributions of firms or plants (that is, differing in both numbers and dispersion). A common solution to this problem is to translate each size distribution into the *equivalent number* of equal-sized firms, and then to record as more concentrated the market with fewer equivalent firms. The equivalent number for any distribution depends on the concentration index employed, but a common feature is that larger firms are weighted more heavily because of their presumed greater effect on the degree of competition. The well-known Herfindahl index may be used in this way and a generalised version of this, as suggested by Hannah and Kay (1977), is:

$$N(a) = \sum^{N} (s_i^a)^{1/(1-a)} \tag{8}$$

where s_i is the market share of firm i and a is a parameter (chosen by the researcher) with larger a values indicating a higher weight attached to large firms in translating the size distribution into an equivalent number of equal-sized firms.

Similarly, if we then divide aggregate market size by $N(a)$, we have a measure of *average effective firm size*. Loosely speaking, this is a weighted average firm size, with larger weights attached to the sizes of the bigger firms. In most actual industries, comprising firms of very different sizes, this reasonably represents typical size as depending mainly on the sizes of those firms responsible for the lion's share of output. (Arithmetic mean size, on the other hand, may diverge greatly from typical size in an industry comprising a few large dominant firms and hundreds of very small ones.)

The relevance of these considerations is obvious if (4) is compared with

(8): measuring the size of plants by employment, $s_i = L_i/L$. P is the aforesaid average effective *plant* size, with the a parameter equal to $\alpha + \beta$, the extent of returns to scale.

Turning to the measurement of P, we encounter a problem in that α and β must be known in order to compute the variable. In general, we do not have this information, and this forces us to seek an easily measurable proxy. As it happens, there exists an excellent candidate, a measure widely used in many studies of 'typical' plant size (for example, Sargant Florence, 1972; Prais, 1976). This is the *median of the first moment plant size distribution*, that is, the midpoint plant size in the sense that 50 per cent of industry employment is accounted for by plants of less than that size. Intuitively this can be justified by the fact that the midpoint (designated below by PM) offers a good approximation to P.

If the logarithm of plant size in a given industry is normally distributed (as is often approximately the case) with mean μ and variance σ^2, then from Aitchison's and Brown's (1957, Chapter 2) summary of the moments of the lognormal, we know that

$$PM = exp\{\mu + \sigma^2\}$$
$$L \equiv N\bar{L} = N exp\{\mu + (1/2)\sigma^2\}$$
$$\text{and} \sum(\frac{L_i}{L})^{\alpha+\beta} = N^{1-(\alpha+\beta)} exp\{(1/2)\sigma^2(\alpha+\beta)(\alpha+\beta-1)\}$$

In these circumstances (4) is:

$$P = exp\{\mu + (1/2)\sigma^2(\alpha+\beta-1)\} \text{ and so}$$
$$P = PM\{(1/2)\sigma^2(\alpha+\beta-1)\}$$

Therefore the use of PM to proxy P involves a measurement error which depends on the magnitude of $(1/2)\sigma^2(\alpha+\beta-1)$; clearly this error is smaller the less pronounced is dispersion (σ^2) and the more nearly constant are returns to scale $(\alpha+\beta = 1)$. In fact there are good reasons for supposing that the effect of this error in equation (6) is likely to be unimportant. Substituting the comparative form of (4) and (6) and taking logarithms, we derive a linear relation between VPW and EFF, CAP and comparative PM plus an additional term:

$$(1/2)(\alpha+\beta-1)^2(\sigma_K^2 - \sigma_S^2)$$

Since typical values of $\alpha + \beta$ are likely to cluster around unity, $(\alpha+\beta-1)^2$ is likely to be very small, and, even were this not the case, a significant inter-country difference in the dispersion of plant sizes in the industry would be required for this term to be of any magnitude. (Since the dispersion of plants should be determined largely by technological factors common to both countries, this is also unlikely.)[4]

INCORPORATING DIFFERENCES IN HUMAN CAPITAL

In the model developed so far, the labour force has been treated as a homogeneous input. The evidence reviewed in Chapter 1 suggested that low inputs of human capital may well prove important for explaining low productivity in Britain, so we shall want to incorporate differences between the matched industries in their human capital inputs as fully as possible. The incidence of part-time working and the proportions of the production and non-production workers in the labour force are among the variables widely recognised as capturing differences in human capital inputs. The female proportion of the workforce also plays this role, because of the disadvantages that women face in securing training, accumulating on-the-job experience, and maintaining continuity of employment.

In order to allow for differences in labour 'quality' among industries and between the two countries, we now replace L in the production function with L', labour measured in efficiency units. Suppose initially that there are two types of labour, say males (L_M) and females (L_F). We define L' by:

$$L' = L_M + \lambda L_F \text{ where } \lambda \gtrless 1 \text{ and } L_M + L_F \equiv L \qquad (9)$$

If f is the proportion of females in the work force $(L_F/L = f)$, then

$$Y = AK^{\alpha}L^{\beta}(1 - f + \lambda f)^{\beta} \qquad (10)$$

As can be seen, this results in an additional term in the production function. In order to derive the implications for our estimating equation, we must express (10) in comparative British/American form (assuming that f is reasonably constant among plants within each country) and take logarithms. This process results in an extra explanatory variable:

$$\beta[\log(1 - f_K + \lambda f_K) - \log(1 - f_S + \lambda f_S)]$$

This expression is unobservable as it stands, because it depends on the unknown λ. However, so long as $(\lambda - 1)f$ is small, then using the approximation x for $\log(1 + x)$, this term can be approximated by:

$$\beta(\lambda - 1)(f_K - f_S)$$

In other words, we can approximately control for the different unobserved human capital or 'quality' between males and females by including the explanatory variable $(f_K - f_S)$. If women possess lower stocks of training and job-related capital than men, we might expect that $\lambda < 1$, and the variable would attract a negative regression coefficient.

We shall wish to control for a number of differences in labour quality or human capital endowments, not just one, and so we need to generalise this result. Consider the randomly selected worker who possesses c characteristics that affect the number of 'efficiency units' that he or she embodies. The 'efficiency units' rating of the worker is:

$$\{(1-p_1)+\lambda_1 p_1\}\{1-p_2)+\lambda_2 p_2\} \ldots \tag{11}$$

$$= \prod_{j=1}^{c} \{1+(\lambda_j-1)p_j\}$$

where p_j is the probability that a worker will exhibit characteristic j and λ_j reflects the efficiency differential of a worker with characteristic j over one without it (so $\lambda_j \geq 1$, depending on the nature of the characteristic). Substituting (11) into (10) in place of $(1-f+\lambda f)$, and assuming that each of the $(\lambda_j-1)p_j$ is small, generates c further explanatory variables in the estimating equations:

$$\sum_{j=1}^{c} \beta(\lambda_j-1)(p_{Kj}-p_{Sj})$$

where p now refers to the empirically observed frequencies of each characteristic. Several dichotomised characteristics will be proposed for this treatment in our model; the proportions of women, part-time workers, non-production employees, and managers in the workforce.

Notice that, in order to derive such a convenient generalisation, we have assumed (in equation 11) that the c characteristics are independent of each other. As the preceding list immediately suggests, this is at best a rough approximation. A more precise formulation would require that we introduce conditional probabilities, which correspond to empirical magnitudes that are difficult to observe on the full sample of industries. The main effect of the independence assumption being violated will be to complicate the interpretation of the estimated regression coefficients[5] rather than to entail the omission of variables. We remain hopeful that our approach provides a satisfactory control for labour quality differences taken as a whole.

IMPACT OF LABOUR RELATIONS ON PRODUCTIVITY

A central concern in our pursuit of influences on relative British/American efficiency will be the role of labour relations, and they pose certain problems for consistent treatment in the context of our core neoclassical model. Antagonistic labour relations can impair productivity either through strikes or through limiting the output obtained from those hours actually worked. Output is lost when strikes occur, both directly through foregone labour input and through various indirect channels. Divisive labour relations may exact various costs not directly associated with strike activity, as a result of restrictive work rules, disincentives to cooperation, and various costs incurred defensively by business managers. These possibilities raise a series of issues for the specification of our model. We take these up in turn.

Direct and indirect costs of strikes

With labour productivity measured conventionally as net output per employee per year, we can regard its impairment due to strikes, as a first approximation, as proportional to the labour services withheld during the course of industrial disputes. However, that proportionality could fail to hold for diverse reasons. Especially if strikes are a ritualised form of industrial protest, it may be that the tacit accord between management and labour allows for the lost output to be partly replaced in a subsequent catch-up. Alternatively, strikes may indicate (or leave behind) a reservoir of ill-will and non-cooperation and thus proxy a state of adversary and counterproductive labour relations. Or strikes may simply have adverse effects on the productivity of workers not involved, or impose extra costs due to the shut-down and start-up of production that inflate the cost in foregone output. Such 'knock-on' effects and incidental costs would make the loss of output more than proportional to the working time lost due to strikes.

We need to consider the implication of these catch-up and knock-on effects for the formulation of our model. Suppose, first, that neither is present, and that x lost working days have the same effect whether one worker is on strike for x days or x workers are on strike for one day. Then the relationship between the effective labour services L' obtained by a given industry and the reported size of its workforce (L) is:

$$L' = \lambda L \text{ where } \lambda = 1 - WDL/LX$$

with WDL standing for working days lost and X being the average number of days in a working year. In the context of our production-function approach, the relation between output, capital, and labour services (with constant returns to scale assumed for expository simplicity) is:

$$Y = AK^a L'^{1-a}$$

and so we can write

$$Y/L = A(K/L)^a L^{a-1} L'^{1-a} = A(K/L)^a \lambda^{1-a} \tag{12}$$

Thus, labour productivity measured per worker-year is inversely related to normalised WDL.

We can generalise the relation $L' = \lambda L$ as $\lambda^\theta L$, where $\theta > 1$ implies that lost labour services are understated by WDL/LX, that is, knock-on effects; and $\theta < 1$ implies catching-up effects (remember that $\lambda < 1$). The corresponding revision to equation (12) is:

$$Y/L = A(K/L)^a \lambda^{(1-a)\theta} \tag{12a}$$

With the production function expressed in comparative, logarithmic terms, this formulation generates an extra variable in the production function:

$$\log\{(1 - WDL/LX)_K/(1 - WDL/LX)_S\} \tag{13}$$

Its regression coefficient is an estimate of $(1 - a)\theta$, which allows us (given that an estimate of a is generated elsewhere in the regression) to test for knock-on and catch-up effects.

This expression for the cost of work lost due to strikes fails, however, to make maximal use of the available information. Suppose that a stoppage has an adverse effect on the productivity of workers not directly involved in the strike-afflicted plant. Specifically, assume that, for each day of strike, the labour services of uninvolved workers are reduced by k per cent. Then, for plant i, the annual direct loss is WDL_i and the indirect loss is $k(D_iL_i - WDL_i)$ where D_i is the number of strike afflicted days and L_i is the total workforce of the plant.

Summing over the N plants in the industry, the total loss is:

$$\Sigma WDL_i + k\Sigma(D_iL_i - WDL_i) = WDL[(1 - k) + (k\Sigma D_iL_i)/WDL] \tag{14}$$

Assuming no tendency for larger plants to have longer strikes, we can write $k\Sigma D_iL_i = kd\Sigma s_iL_i$ where d is the average duration of a strike and s_i is the number of strikes in plant i. If, moreover, larger plants have no tendency to incur more strikes,[6] $\Sigma s_iL_i = (S/N)L$ where S and L are the total number of strikes and employees in the industry, and N is the number of plants.

Under these circumstances, (12) can be rewritten:

$$WDL[(1 - k) + kdLS/(WDL)N]$$

Then, noting that $WDL = dWI$, where $WI =$ the number of workers directly involved in strikes, and normalising WDL as above, we find that the proportionate loss of labour services is:

$$\frac{WDL}{LX}\left[(1 - k) + k\{(\tfrac{S}{N})/(\tfrac{WI}{L})\}\right] \tag{14a}$$

In other words, for given WDL/LX, the loss is greater the smaller is the proportion of workers in an average plant directly involved in each strike. By implication, two separate strikes each involving 50 per cent of the workers in a plant will be worse than one strike of equal duration involving all workers.

Although expression (14a) utilises information on each magnitude of strike activity reported in official statistics, k is unknown and so we are unable to enter this index as a single variable in our regression equations. Instead, we opt for a second-best specification by including two explanatory variables multiplicatively, the days-lost variable (equation 13) and the ratio of the proportion of workers involved in stoppages to the number of strikes per plant. In logged comparative form, the latter becomes:

$$\log\{(WI/L)(S/N)_K/(WI/L)(S/N)_S\} \tag{15}$$

Our model leads us to expect a positive coefficient for this variable when it is included alongside (13).

Disruption to production lines

A further cost due to strikes may lie in the fixed expense of closing down and restarting operations, including the disruption of production runs and the loss of learning effects. Suppose that the representative firm wishes to organise its production in runs of Z' units of output, that is, at the foot of the following curve:

$$w = aZ^{-b} \text{ for } Z < Z', b > 0$$

where w is labour input per unit of output and Z is the length of the run. But suppose that there are s stoppages (at equal intervals) in the time needed for a complete run. So in place of one run of Z', the plant obtains $s+1$ runs of $Z'/(s+1)$. Productivity, which free of stoppages is $a^{-1}(Z')^b$, is reduced to

$$[a^{-1}(Z')^b](s+1)^{-b}$$

Thus, stoppages reduce productivity by a factor which is quantitatively more important the more frequent are stoppages. For each plant, then, the frequency of strikes should proxy the fixed-cost element.

These considerations call for the simple proxy

$$S/N \tag{16}$$

the number of stoppages normalised by the number of plants. Theory does not establish whether the comparative form of this variable should be specified as the logarithm of the United Kingdom/United States ratio or as the arithmetic difference.

Uncertainty

The losses discussed so far are incurred by stoppages and large even if those stoppages are anticipated by management. But it is often argued that the uncertain frequency and timing of strikes impose extra costs, as firms commit resources to mitigate the consequences of strikes for continuity in production and delivery. As we mentioned in Chapter 1, these extra costs can take the forms of excess capacity or inventories, extra managerial specialists in labour relations, and the like.

The essence of the problem is captured in the following simple example. A firm is committed to producing X units in the coming year. Each of its workers produces 1 unit per day on each of 250 working days. So, without strikes, the firm needs $X/250$ workers. Now suppose that the firm knows with certainty that strikes will occur on Y days (each involving complete shutdown). If so, it must employ a labour force of $X/(250-Y)$. The impairment of productivity is simply proportional to the idle time due to strikes. But now introduce uncertainty about the number of strikes: while the expectation is still Y, there is now a variance of σ^2 about this mean. One way the firm might react is to carry sufficient resources (including labour) to attain its production target with 95 per cent probability. Suppose that the probability distribution of strike frequency is normal. Then the number of strikes will exceed the following number with only 5 per cent probability:

$$Y + 1.645\,\sigma$$

and so the labour force should be:

$$X(250 - Y - 1.645\,\sigma)^{-1}$$

This inflated workforce will enable the target to be met with 95 per cent probability, but, except when the actual number of stoppages approaches the upper limit, a significant proportion of it (along with cooperating resources) will be under-employed throughout the year even on strike-free days.

What little research has been done on strike frequencies in fact suggests a Poisson rather than a normal probability distribution (Kendall, 1961, and Prais, 1978). Nevertheless, the variance remains an obvious candidate for representing the degree of uncertainty. In general, there would be little hope of estimating the variance at the individual plant level from published data, but this is where we benefit from a lucky coincidence: the mean and variance of the Poisson distribution are identical. Since Prais (1981, Chapter 7) has shown that the number of strikes in a plant employing n workers approximates to an, where a is fairly constant across plants, the expected number of strikes in the industry-average sized plant is an, which can be estimated by the number of stoppages in the industry (S) deflated by the number of plants. This is exactly expression (16), derived above to capture the effect of disruption due to strikes. On the assumptions made here, it also reflects the typical variance of expected output at the plant level.

The atmosphere of labour relations

Even with the preceding aspects of labour controlled, we still need to allow for the tone of day-to-day relations between labour and management, which may be degraded to varying degrees by a prevailing atmosphere of resentment, unrest, and lack of cooperation. The importance of this factor is underlined by the widespread recognition that official disputes data in Britain reflect only the 'tip of the iceberg.' It is well known in both Britain and America that many strikes are not recorded,[7] and that strikes blur indistinguishably into go-slows, work-to-rules, and the like.

How can we use observable data to measure the prevailing (dis)harmony of labour relations in a given industry? A procedure that suggests itself is an extension of the model developed by Prais (1981, Chapter 7). Consider a plant i, organised on hierarchical lines with L_i employees, K_i levels of management or supervision, and a span of control c. Prais showed that the number of pairwise contacts among employees in such a plant is:

$$N_i = (L_i - 1)(c + 1)/2$$

Now assume that there is a small probability, p, that any one contact or encounter will cast up a conflict resulting in a strike. If so, the expected number of strikes is

$$S_i \simeq aL_i, \text{ where } a = p(c + 1)/2$$

aggregating across all plants in the industry, $S/L = a$. If we accept that p is a reasonable measure of the degree of disharmony in labour relations, then, so long as c is roughly constant across plants and industries, inter-industry variations in a should indicate inter-industry differences in what Prais called 'the degree of bellicosity,' and S/L will serve as an indicator.

For our purposes this model benefits from two extensions. First, we do not wish to impose the assumption of strict proportionality between strikes and plant size, and therefore substitute the more general form

$$S_i = aL_i^{\beta} \text{ where } \beta \gtrless 1 \tag{17}$$

Second, and more important, the probability of conflict p may differ systematically among industries in association with the character of the workplace and the workforce. For example, while human relations involving non-unionised/female/white-collar workers may be no more harmonious than those involving blue-collar unionised males, there is at least the possibility that workers with one or more of the former set of characteristics are less disposed to strike.

This suggests a method for inferring inter-industry differences in bellicosity that cannot be observed directly. Expression (16), strikes per plant, can be written as an aggregation across plants of equation (17):

$$S/N = a(N)^{-1} \Sigma L_i^{\beta}$$

Although $N^{-1} \Sigma L_i^{\beta}$ is not strictly observable because β is unknown, it is clearly related to the typical size of plant in the industry, and we shall suppose that it can be approximated by our plant-size proxy, P. We assume that a can be explained by a linear combination of labour-force characteristics and BEL, an unobservable index of disharmony in the industry's labour relations. Then we can employ an estimating equation in the form

$$S/N = a_0 + a_1 \log P + a_2 BEL + \Sigma a_i Z_i \tag{18}$$

where the Z_i are a series of characteristics such as the proportions of females, part-time workers, union members, and non-production workers in the industry's labour force. These variables are measurable in principle except, of course, for *BEL*. When we estimate equation (18) with *BEL* omitted, we generate a set of residuals that should reflect, to a greater or lesser extent, inter-industry differences in *BEL*. We shall estimate equation (18) separately for the United Kingdom and United States and take the difference between them as our estimate of the relative disharmony of labour relations in the British industry.

3

DETERMINANTS OF RELATIVE EFFICIENCY

In this chapter we describe the database that was assembled to test our model of the determinants of relative productivity. The model was developed as a cross-section, and its logic calls for estimating it with comparable data for the United Kingdom and United States pertaining to some common year in which the two economies were relatively free of major short-run disturbances. We in fact chose two years, 1967/8 and 1977, for several reasons: to assess the robustness of the results, to check for any evidence of trends that a two-point observation might be able to suggest, and to set the scene for the analysis of comparative productivity growth over this period (Chapter 6).

The years selected were importantly constrained by the data that are available. The United States Census of Manufactures is taken only every fifth year, as was the United Kingdom Census of Production before 1970. We wanted observations at least a decade apart, but were denied use of a year after 1977 by the long lag in collecting and publishing many of the relevant data. The year 1972 seemed unattractive because of unusually high levels of activity and the application of price controls in the United States. The years 1967 (United States) and 1968 (United Kingdom) seemed preferable to the remote year of 1963.

We employed the standard industrial classification manuals of the two countries to construct concordances between the British Minimum List Heading industries and the four-digit industries of the American classification for each year.[1] This process yielded a maximum usable number of 86 industries for 1967/8 and 101 for 1977. Typically, one British MLH industry is matched to one or more American four-digit industries, but in some cases we built up groups of industries in both classifications in order to secure a satisfactory match.

ESTIMATION OF THE NEOCLASSICAL CORE MODEL

The estimation procedure developed in Chapter 2 on the basis of a consistent model of production functions takes as its dependent variable

VPW = relative[2] real net output per employee (average number of employees over the year).

In constructing VPW we corrected it for inter-industry differences in relative prices.[3] This important step, not always undertaken in studies of this type, averts the error of (say) presuming that an industry is highly productive when it simply charges a high price for its output.

The foremost neoclassical influence on labour productivity to be controlled is that of capital intensity. We utilise the variable:

CAP = relative gross fixed capital stock per employee.

It should take a positive regression coefficient. The model developed in Chapter 2 also calls for the inclusion of

$CAPK$ = gross fixed capital stock per employee, United Kingdom.

The function of this variable is to allow for any systematic difference in the output-elasticities of capital between the United Kingdom and the United States. No general hypothesis foretells the sign of this variable's coefficient. However, the legendary difficulties with labour relations in Britain and the incentive that they create for the substitution of capital for labour could appear (given the measurement of labour in nominal terms) as an effective shift towards higher capital productivity, implying a positive coefficient.

In Chapter 2 we also showed that the influence of scale economies on relative productivity can be allowed for by incorporating the variable

TP = relative size of the median plant, that is, the plant accounting for the 50 percentile of activity (output or employment), when plants in an industry are ranked from the largest to the smallest.

The sign of this variable should be positive and the coefficient should indicate the extent of economies of scale enjoyed by the typical manufacturing industry. Once again, we should allow for the possibility that the same scale economies are not effectively available to the typical British industry as to its counterpart in the United States. The model therefore includes

TPK = size of the median plant, British industry.

Should British plant sizes be small enough for expansion to yield substantial scale economies, while American plants have largely exhausted them, the variable's coefficient will be positive. On the other hand, the discussion in Chapter 1 raised the possibility of a negative coefficient, reflecting the conjunction of ineffective management and divisive labour relations in large plants.

Just as $CAPK$ and TPK allow for generic differences in manufacturing production functions between the United Kingdom and the United States, we also need to make what allowance we can for differences between industries. In Chapter 2 we showed that this can be done with slope-shift variables that permit CAP and TP to take different slopes where we expect either scale economies or the output-elasticity of capital to be substantially larger or smaller than in the typical manufacturing industry. These differences are a matter of technology and not economic behaviour, and so we had to proceed inductively. The statistical results reported below will reveal what sectors we found to differ significantly in scale economies and output elasticities.

The remaining variables that enter the neoclassical core of the model are those relating to human capital or qualitative properties of the labour force. Four variables in the form of UK/US differences seem appropriate to capture variations in these endowments between the matched industries:

$PCF=$ difference in the female proportions of the workforce

$PART=$ difference in the proportions of the workforce employed on a part-time basis

$NOPS=$ difference in the proportions of the workforce not directly engaged in production activities

ED = difference in the average number of years of formal schooling of the workforce.[4]

$PART$ should take a negative coefficient, being simply a correction for the measurement of labour input by numbers of employees rather than employee-hours. On the usual presumptions about differences in acquired skills and training, the coefficient of PCF should be negative and those of $NOPS$ and ED should be positive. One potentially important dimension of relative labour quality is unfortunately missed by these variables; the extent of vocational and craft education outside of formal schooling. Evidence cited in Chapter 1 raises the possibility that Britain significantly under-invests in this type of training, at least relative to Germany. We lack evidence that would permit a similar comparison to the United States.

Table 3.1 reports several estimates of this neoclassical core of our model for 1967/8 and 1977. Equation 1 represents the logarithmic regression of VPW on only CAP and TP. The coefficient of CAP is positive and significant in both years. The coefficient of TP is also positive and significant in 1977, although not in 1968. When $CAPK$ and TPK are added in equation 2, we find no significant difference in capital productivity between the two countries. However, TPK takes a negative coefficient that is statistically significant in a two-tail test in both years. It approximately offsets the scale economies that the model indicates (for 1977, at least) are enjoyed by the typical American industry. This result provides forceful evidence that something is amiss with productivity in large plants in Britain, that either technology or economic organisation yields smaller economies of scale than in the United States.

The estimated elasticities of output with respect to capital are in the range of 10 to 15 per cent in 1967/8, 17 to 27 per cent in 1977. The data for 1967/8 reveal no appreciable scale economies in the typical industry, but those for 1977 indicate a range of 6 to 8 per cent, typical of values reported in similar studies using data for single countries (for example, Griliches and Ringstad, 1971). Equation 3 indicates the evidence that we found of inter-

Table 3.1. *Estimates of determinants of VPW, 1967/8 and 1977, neoclassical core model*

Independent variable	Equation (1) 1967/8	1977	Equation (2) 1967/8	1977	Equation (3) 1967/8	1977	Equation (4) 1967/8	1977
Constant	-0.833^{aa}	-0.769^{aa}	-0.363^{bb}	-0.309^{bb}	-0.468^{aa}	-0.291^{bb}	-0.126	-0.367^{bb}
	(17.70)	(21.61)	(2.37)	(2.11)	(3.57)	(2.04)	(0.93)	(2.53)
log CAP	0.104^{a}	0.265^{a}	0.075^{b}	0.173^{a}	0.130^{a}	0.202^{a}	0.150^{a}	0.210^{a}
	(2.42)	(5.07)	(1.65)	(3.25)	(3.10)	(3.56)	(3.95)	(3.47)
log TP	-0.019	0.063^{a}	0.024	0.079^{a}	-0.004	0.077^{a}		
	(0.50)	(3.27)	(0.63)	(4.03)	(0.12)	(3.57)		
log CAPK			-0.043	0.033				
			(1.30)	(1.07)				
log TPK			-0.074^{aa}	-0.091^{aa}	-0.055^{bb}	-0.080^{aa}	-0.051^{bb}	-0.041^{cc}
			(2.72)	(4.10)	(2.40)	(3.50)	(2.31)	(1.83)
log CHECAP					0.310^{aa}	0.117	0.324^{aa}	0.096
					(3.87)	(0.125)	(4.66)	(1.00)
log ELCAP					-0.122^{bb}	-0.192^{cc}	-0.143^{aa}	-0.226^{bb}
					(2.25)	(1.85)	(2.92)	(2.08)
log BMCAP					-0.160^{aa}	-0.203^{cc}	-0.144^{aa}	-0.221^{cc}
					(2.76)	(1.74)	(2.84)	(1.83)
log ELTP					0.324^{aa}	0.068	0.348^{aa}	0.127^{aa}
					(3.03)	(1.48)	(3.92)	(2.91)
PCF							-0.421^{b}	-0.105
							(2.14)	(0.43)
PART							-1.136^{a}	-1.242^{a}
							(3.65)	(3.00)
NOPS							-0.465^{bb}	-0.077
							(2.00)	(0.25)
ED							0.143^{a}	0.073^{b}
							(3.40)	(1.69)
R^2	0.081	0.248	0.208	0.368	0.463	0.423	0.621	0.407
$\bar{R}^2$	0.055	0.231	0.162	0.339	0.406	0.377	0.561	0.336
F	3.14	14.98	4.52	12.95	8.13	9.04	10.31	5.71

Notes: The number of observations is 74 for 1967/8 and 94 for 1977, reduced from 86 and 101 respectively due to missing observations in *CAP* or *TP* for one or the other country. T-statistics appear in parentheses beneath the coefficients. Levels of statistical significance: where one-tail tests are appropriate, a = 1 per cent, b = 5 per cent, c = 10 per cent; where two-tail tests are appropriate, aa = 1 per cent, bb = 5 per cent, cc = 10 per cent.

sectoral differences in the output elasticities. Our choice of broad sectors for which we applied the slope-shift variables was initially confined to chemicals, metals, engineering, and textiles and clothing (the first three apparently employing more capital-intensive, and the last less capital-intensive technologies than the typical manufacturing industry). Subsequently, we extended these experiments in a limited way by splitting the largest groups of industries. The statistical results in table 3.1 show that the effect of capital-intensity is especially strong in the chemicals industries (*CHECAP*) but weak in building materials (*BMCAP*) and electrical and instrument engineering ($ELCAP$). Scale economies, however, seem to be more pronounced in the electrical and instrument engineering sector ($ELTP$).[5] Although the coefficients differ substantially between the two years, we found no evidence of changes in the sectors for which significant differences are observed.

Equation 4 brings the human-capital variables into the model. The coefficients of $PART$ and ED are significant and take the expected signs. The coefficient of PCF is negative as expected although significant only for 1967/8. That for the difference in the proportions of non-production employees is surprisingly negative and statistically significant for 1967/8. Although non-operative employees include a wide variety of skill levels (managers, research staff, technicians, lorry drivers, canteen workers), non-production workers on average are normally found to be both higher skilled and higher paid than production workers. It may be that the skill mixtures possessed by non-production workers differ significantly between Britain and America, and that relatively low British wages encounter an elastic demand for low-skill classes of non-production workers (for example, canteen workers, maintenance and cleaning staff). It may also be that 'excess' workers of these types serve as perquisites and non-pecuniary compensation for other employees, both production workers and executives; one cannot avoid raising the question whether social custom in providing compensation in this form might be inefficient for all concerned, with pounds in the pay packet traded gladly for tea servers if the question were tactfully put.

The explanatory power of the neoclassical core model is quite substantial, relative to one's expectations for a cross-section model expressed in the form of differentials. In equation 4, 56 per cent of the variance is explained for 1967/8 and 34 per cent for 1977.

HYPOTHESES RELATING TO EFFICIENCY DIFFERENCES

The core model that was estimated in table 3.1 derives from equation 6 in Chapter 2, which we repeat here:

$$VPW_j = EFF_j * CAP_j{}^a * TP_j{}^{a+\beta-1}$$

We now turn to specifying what lies behind the catch-all term for relative efficiency, EFF. At this stage we gather in the main bodies of hypotheses reviewed in Chapter 1: British management may be at fault; the blame may lie with labour attitudes and the degenerate bargain struck between management and labour; and industrial organisation factors may be at issue, with British plants too small (or too large given potential problems of labour relations) or British markets insufficiently competitive to attain high levels of efficiency.

The managerial factor

The hypothesis that British management is ineffective raises interesting tactical problems for our statistical test. In an earlier study (Caves, 1980), the hypothesis was embodied in the specific prediction that productivity is lower in Britain in those industries that employ relatively large proportions of skilled managers in the United States. That prediction was confirmed in the statistical results. However, the finding may be given two interpretations that differ greatly in their implications for policy. It may be that entrepreneurship simply suffers from some cultural inhibition in Britain, implying no ready solution other than the transfer of resources towards sectors that place only modest demands on entrepreneurial capacity. Or it may be that Britain simply under-invests in managerial skills or that British enterprises employ too few managerial personnel.

We can discriminate between these two interpretations by formulating the following variable:

MGR = difference between managers and kindred employees as a proportion of total employees.

Caves (1980) found that VPW was negatively related to the United States level, $MGRS$. If MGR itself does not attract a significant positive coefficient, we conclude that the 'managerial failure' hypothesis cannot be rejected. If MGR's coefficient is significant, then we cannot reject the hypothesis that Britain underprovides managerial personnel.[6]

Some other avenues are available for investigating managerial performance. The evidence cited in Chapter 1 suggested that the under-performance of British management is evident in the differential success of multinational companies, suggesting the hypothesis that productivity might be higher in British industries populated by larger numbers of foreign-controlled companies. We use:

$FOSK$ = proportion of industry sales in Britain accounted for by companies classed as foreign controlled.

The hypothesis suggests a positive regression coefficient.

Another often cited hypothesis in the general area of management concerns the possibility that research and development is somehow managed in an inferior way in Britain. The case studies described by Pavitt (1980), for example, are highly suggestive in this respect. Two aspects of this problem can be handled within our framework. First, is it the case that British industry simply spends too little on R&D? If it does, and if the shortfall varies somewhat between industries, we should expect that VPW is positively related to:

RD = difference between research and development expenditures as a proportion of sales in Britain and the American counterpart industry.

Secondly, but not necessarily alternatively, it may be that the research-intensive industry is one that requires substantial and especially effective managerial inputs, so that British managerial shortcomings are most sharply exposed. This hypothesis can be tested by allowing the regression coefficient of MGR to vary depending on the research intensity of the industry. This requires an additional explanatory variable:

$MGRRDK = MGR$ multiplied by the ratio of R & D expenditures to sales in the British industry.

A negative coefficient is predicted.

Labour relations

Both countries collect industry-level data on three dimensions of industrial disputes: number of stoppages, working days lost due to strikes, and numbers of workers involved in strikes. It is common practice, especially in the literature on industrial relations, to use some sort of *ad hoc* weighted average to summarise these three aspects of labour disputes. We showed in Chapter 2, however, that this procedure misses several subtle aspects of the problem of representing the effect of industrial relations problems on productivity.

First, working days lost due to strikes can be viewed as simply a deduction from the working-years of labour input utilised by an industry. This could be accomplished by multiplying our figures on the labour input by a factor representing the proportion of employee days worked (which assumes that a day lost has just that effect on the input, that is, one less day is inputted). In comparative terms, this means that the UK/US labour-input ratio should be multiplied by

WDL = relative (UK/US) proportion of working days actually worked (that is, the proportion of days *not* lost due to strikes).

More generally, however, working days lost may interact with the state of an industry's labour relations in specific ways, either through 'catching up' effects when production lost through strikes can, by mutual consent, be made up later; or by 'knock-on' effects when the ramifications of the strike may impair productivity in periods following (and perhaps preceding) the stoppage. These possibilities can be captured by including WDL as an additional explanatory variable with no restriction on its coefficient.[7] Alternatively, a slightly more elegant way to model the phenomenon of knock-ons is to permit the productivity of workers uninvolved in strikes to be impaired. We showed in Chapter 2 that this requires the addition of:

$STCOV$ = relative proportion of the workforce involved in the average strike (it is derived as the ratio of the proportion of workers involved in strikes to the number of strikes per plant).

Included alongside WDL, $STCOV$ should have a positive impact on VPW because, for a given number of days lost in strikes, the detrimental productivity effect is reduced if the days are lost in a few large strikes rather than many small ones.

Secondly, it is often argued that the main cost of strikes is not so much the loss of days as the disruption of production lines and the uncertainty which arises about the output that the plant can deliver. We showed in Chapter 2 that these two effects are best captured by data on the number of stoppages normalised by the number of plants in the industry:

$STRIK$ = difference in the average number of strikes per plant.

With WDL controlled, a negative coefficient of $STRIK$ indicates the incidental disruption and transactions costs imposed by divisive industrial relations.

Thirdly, and for some commentators the most significant consideration, the underlying atmosphere of labour relations may vitally affect productivity. On this view, information on industrial disputes is interesting not so much for its own sake but for what it reveals about the nature of day-to-day relations between labour and management. Work stoppages and impaired productivity then become joint consequences of the unobserved resentment and hostility that colours the industry's labour relations. In Chapter 2 we set forth a method for digging out the unobserved variable by means of an extension of Prais's (1981, Chapter 7) model of the incidence of strikes, which he related to the number of pairwise communications or contacts between persons in a hierarchical organisation. Measuring the inherent 'degree of bellicosity' in an organisation by the probability that any given contact may result in a work stoppage, he showed that this may be estimated for a given industry by the number of stoppages per employee.

We extended this model to show that the frequency of strikes in an industry should depend not only on the bellicosity of its labour relations but also on a number of observable attributes of its labour force and technology, including those captured in Prais's model. Empirically, the model implies that we can estimate the determinants of the variable $STRIK$ and take the residuals from it as an estimate of the bellicosity of labour relations in each country.

Table 3.2 reports the regression models from which this variable, designated BEL, was taken. $STRIKK$ was regressed on independent variables pertaining to the United Kingdom, and $STRIKS$ in turn on independent variables for the United States. The regressors used in the models include the logarithm of typical plant size (TP), the female proportion of the labour force (PCF), the proportion of non-production workers ($NOPS$), and the proportion of part-time employees ($PART$) (the latter two variables proved significant, and were utilised, only for 1977). The proportion of employees who are union members ($UNION$) is entered both in its natural form and squared, because the underlying theory set forth in Prais's model emphasises conflict between unionised and non-

Table 3.2 *Explanations of strike activity (strikes per establishment) utilised to generate* BEL, *United Kingdom and United States*, 1967/8 *and* 1977

Independent variable	STRIKK		STRIKS	
	1967/8	1977	1967/8	1977
Constant	−0.092	0.518	−0.034	−0.036
	(0.68)	(0.57)	(0.83)	(0.65)
Log TPK/S	0.060^a	0.044^a	0.012^b	0.023^a
	(3.98)	(6.36)	(2.49)	(4.00)
$PCFK/S$	-0.147^a	−0.028	−0.022	-0.101^b
	(2.49)	(0.44)	(0.94)	(2.06)
$UNIONK/S$	−0.515	−0.787	−0.117	0.388
	(0.94)	(2.50)	(1.42)	(2.35)
$(UNIONK/S)^2$	0.556	0.804^{aa}	0.191^{bb}	-0.293^{bb}
	(1.14)	(2.80)	(2.53)	(2.01)
$NOPK/S$		-0.156^b		-0.185^a
		(2.00)		(2.47)
$PARTK/S$		-0.337^c		−0.101
		(1.58)		(0.85)
R^2	0.429	0.498	0.426	0.304
$\bar{R}^2$	0.400	0.464	0.393	0.256
F	12.94	14.41	12.91	6.32

Note: Independent variables pertain to United Kingdom industries (K) when the dependent variable is *STRIKK*: to United States industries (S) when it is *STRIKS*. Levels of statistical significance: where one-tail tests are appropriate, a = 1 per cent, b = 5 per cent, c = 10 per cent; where two-tail tests are appropriate, aa = 1 per cent, bb = 5 per cent, cc = 10 per cent.

union employees as one possible source of strikes. The proportion of the variance of *STRIK* explained is in each case substantial but not 'very large,' stirring the reasonable expectation that *BEL*, the difference between British and American residuals from these models, may contain useful information about the varying levels of underlying antagonism in industries' labour relations. As to the regression models themselves, the coefficients of *TP*, *PCF*, *NOPS*, and *PART* all take the expected signs. The signs of the coefficients of *UNION* and its square, however, do not suggest an interior maximum except in the case of the United States in 1977; a simple linear relation between *STRIK* and *UNION* in each case obtains a significant positive coefficient.

The final variable included to represent the state of labour relations is
UNION = difference between proportions of employees who are union members.

We impose no prior expectation concerning its sign. Unions evidently may provide a vehicle for the imposition of restrictive practices not captured in the variables already specified, indicating a negative coefficient. However, some research on labour relations in the United States has concluded that unions can raise productivity by providing a channel of 'voice' for conveying workers' dissatisfactions and allowing the realisation of productivity improvements that yield a net gain to employer and employees together (Brown and Medoff, 1978). Also, union membership seems more common among skilled employees, and an apparent positive influence of union membership could arise because it proxies skills that are measured inaccurately by other variables in the model.

Industrial organisation and competition

The final group of potential determinants of efficiency addresses the relative degrees of competition in British and American industries. The relation between competitive conditions in an industry and its productivity is not well established in scholarly research. In general, we expect that competition will limit the degree to which inefficient enterprises are viable in the market, that is, able to cover their costs. The popular suspicion that 'monopolists' are inefficient due to a lack of competitive pressure is ultimately not very satisfying. It fails to explain why the monopolist should pass up opportunities to obtain maximum profits. More forcefully, it fails to address the situations of actual industrial markets in which the typical participant invariably faces some threat from actual and potential competitors: do ten rivals impel the firm to minimise its costs, although five do not? On firmer footing is the charge that efficiency and productivity may suffer in concentrated industries because of the form taken by collusive behaviour and tacit or explicit collusive bargains. We know that horizontal collusive agreements among firms, before they came to be restricted by competition policy in the late 1950s, were associated with wide dispersions of productivity levels among competing firms (Downie, 1958) and with substantial excess capacity that was subsequently shaken out as these agreements were abandoned (Swann *et at.*, 1974, Chapter 4). Although such agreements are not necessarily extinct in either Britain or America, systematic indicators of their incidence usable in our cross-section research design are obviously non-existent.

Still, a great deal of evidence on industrial organisation in various countries does suggest that the probability that rival sellers can maintain effective collusion becomes appreciable as levels of seller concentration become moderate, and seems to increase with concentration beyond that point. Although high concentration is only a necessary and not a sufficient condition for collusion, we do include in the model:

C_5 = difference between shares of shipments accounted for by the five largest sellers (United Kingdom minus United States).[8]

With *TP* controlled, we expect that C_5 will indicate the potential for degenerate collusive bargains that impair productivity, and thus predict a negative sign. Notice that the (partial) adjustment of the dependent variable, VPW, for differences between British and American relative prices means that a concentrated industry should not appear 'productive' simply because it obtains a high mark-up of price over marginal cost.

A principal limitation of producer concentration for indicating the scope of inefficient collusive dealings is its failure to allow for either the actual competition of overseas rivals or the potential competition of entrants. Incorporating the latter would take us too far afield for the purposes of this project. However, we must allow for international competition, given its eternally controversial status in public policy. We expect an industry's efficiency and productivity to increase with both the extent of import competition that it faces and the degree to which it sells on export markets. To one schooled in the traditional theory of international trade, it may seem odd that an industry might face competitive discipline from foreign rivals *both* in its home market and abroad. However, evidence of substantial amounts of intra-industry trade in manufactures (consistent with the theory of international trade with imperfect competition), throughout the industrial nations, warrants consolidation of the effects on an industry's productivity of international competition both at home and abroad.

A variable that reflects this exposure to international competition is
$IMEX =$ UK/US difference between sums of imports and exports deflated by value of domestic market size.

If exposure to international competition increases an industry's efficiency, this variable should take a positive coefficient.[9] Research on industrial organisation in both Britain and other countries has suggested that the competitive discipline of international trade interacts in its effects with the concentration of domestic producers: the effect of producer concentration is felt to the extent that exposure to international trade is low, and the influence of trade increases with the concentration of domestic producers. A simple way to express this interaction is $COMPK = C_5K/(1 + IMEXK)$ and its counterpart for the United States, and then to employ the variable:
$COMP = COMPK - COMPS$.

This 'adjustment' to concentration depends, as indeed does the competitive discipline of international trade in general, on the firms supplying the imports and providing rivalry in foreign markets being different from the leading producers in the domestic industry. The prevalence of multinational enterprises among the leading firms renders that assumption inaccurate for many British and American industries. We lack comparable data for the two countries that would permit an adjustment for this problem (see Utton, 1982).

Several other aspects of industrial organisation remain to be considered. We expect that the variable TP will control for the general access of British industries to scale economies. However, its sufficiency rests on the assumption that industries' plant sizes are distributed similarly. Other variables can be introduced to test this assumption. We are interested in whether the small-plant end of the size distribution has any distinctive effect. On the one hand, an 'excessive' concentration of small plants may spell costly diseconomies of small scale. On the other, small firms (and plants) may hold seed-bed potential for the development of enterprises and innovations that will be curbed if the small-business sector is somehow shrivelled.[10] It is also possible that the small-business sectors in some industries simply operate on different production functions and perform different functions from the larger units classified to the industry. We define $SMALK$ as the proportion of British industry employment accounted for by plants employing fewer than 50 workers, $SMALS$ as its American counterpart, and form:

$SMAL = SMALK - SMALS$.

No definite prediction holds concerning its sign.

The two remaining hypotheses are last and, probably, also least, because of the conceptual and statistical problems that they pose. The first of these is aggregate industry size. The view is sometimes expressed that British productivity falls short of American levels because United Kingdom manufacturing industries are smaller. This was a common theme in the analysis of early studies in this field (including some of those mentioned at the beginning of Chapter 2). It must be said, however, that this expectation was (and is) justified partly on the basis of misplaced conceptions of economies of scale, for which we may test more correctly by comparing typical *plant* sizes (TP in our notation). Alternatively, one may invoke a static version of Verdoorn's Law, but its conceptual basis is unclear. The best case for a positive (static) influence of market size on productivity probably rests on differences in run lengths and degrees of specialisation. The cost in productivity of short production runs and non-specialised plants seems quite high for small and protected manufacturing sectors such as Australia (Caves, 1984) and Canada (Harris, 1984), and it arguably shades into the hypothesis that cultural and social factors promote 'excess' product differentiation in British markets.[11]

A test of the effect of market size on productivity is, however, difficult to formulate in a way that will avoid the dangers of inbuilt correlation. For instance, were we to include the ratio of UK/US industry production as an explanatory variable, a positive correlation with VPW seems almost certain because the latter is itself the ratio of comparative production to comparative employment. The argument also applies (but with an inbuilt negative effect) if we measure comparative industry size by comparative employment. Our makeshift solution to this problem involves a variable with no theoretical pedigree but at least capable of warding off this problem:

$SIZE=$ average of the ratios of UK/US industry size, measured alternatively by net output and employment.

A positive coefficient is expected.

A similar conflation of dubious hypothesis and dubious data affects the proposition that greater vertical integration allows for economies of both technological and transactional natures. Moreover, the view is held fairly commonly that integration is typically higher in the United States and that this may account for part of the productivity differential. Again, the problem of measurement is severe. The only aspect of vertical integration that is consistently observable across industries is the ratio of value-added to the value of shipments; however, it reflects many influences other than the integration of discrete stages of production. With the variable expressed as a UK/US ratio for matched industries, this problem is somewhat averted, but in this context relative vertical integration,

$VI=$ ratio of net output to gross output in the British industry divided by the same ratio for the counterpart American industry,

can be rearranged to read as the ratio of comparative net output to comparative gross output. Thus, any positive relationship to VPW can be either behavioural or the result of a spurious correlation.

STATISTICAL RESULTS

We now turn to the results of incorporating these determinants of relative efficiency into the core neoclassical model reported in table 3.1. Good research practice normally calls for testing all hypothesised influences on a variable together, so that their interactions are taken fully into account. However, the large number of variables on hand in this study and the avowedly different degrees of conviction carried by their rationales call for a piecemeal treatment initially. We report in turn our findings on the managerial, labour-relations, and competitive factors.

Managerial factors

In table 3.3 we report a series of truncated equations that show the influence of the putative efficiency determinants in the 1967/8 and 1977 cross-section. Each equation also included all the variables listed in table 3.1. However, the magnitudes and significance levels of the variables in the core model proved quite robust in both years to the addition of various combinations of efficiency determinants, and so we suppress their coefficients in order to reduce the clutter of the results.

Equations 1 and 2 report our findings on the managerial variables. The relative utilisation of managerial personnel, MGR, takes the expected positive coefficient, but it is not statistically significant. Thus, the United

Kingdom's productivity shortfall is not the demonstrated result of employing too few managerial personnel. In the earlier version of this study management intensity in the United States (*MGRS*) displayed a significant negative relation to *VPW*, implying that British productivity decreases significantly with an industry's overall management intensity. When we repeat that experiment with the current database (not shown), the coefficient of *MGRS* is negative but no longer statistically significant.

An examination of the correlations between *MGR* and other explanatory variables indicates a potential problem of multicollinearity. In particular, *MGR* and *TPK* are highly correlated, -0.48 for 1967/8 and -0.37 for 1977. This correlation suggests that the managerial shortfall is especially pronounced in large-plant industries. Accordingly, when *TPK* is omitted from the model, *MGR* attracts a much larger coefficient which for 1967/8 is almost statistically significant at the 10 per cent confidence level. We conclude, therefore, that hypotheses about insufficient or inferior British managerial inputs are not proven. There remains, however, more than a suspicion that deficient managerial input is particularly pronounced in large-plant industries, and this may account for part of the significantly negative effect of *TPK* that persists robustly through all versions of our estimating equation.

Another hypothesis can be discarded more easily. For neither year did we find evidence of a beneficial effect on productivity of a high level of foreign ownership of British industry (*FOSK*). Its coefficient is positive but quite insignificant.

A more interesting picture emerges concerning research and development. On the one hand, there is no evidence that shortfalls in managerial inputs have a more serious effect in research-intensive industries. *MGRRDK*'s coefficient is not significant for either year. However, the results do indicate that relative research and development expenditures make a significant contribution to relative productivity. For 1967/8 the finding is quite robust with regard to inclusion of the other managerial variables (compare equations 1 and 2), but in 1977 it proves significant only when the other managerial variables are omitted.

Labour relations

Our model generated a group of statistical hypotheses about the channels through which antagonistic labour relations might affect productivity. Although the derived variables are formally independent in depicting consequences of the state of an industry's labour relations, they can be expected in practice to display some functional overlap. The results are accordingly mixed.

First, and conclusively, neither *WDL* nor *STCOV* is at all significant (they are omitted from the table). Thus there is no evidence that the sheer loss of labour time through strikes, or related knock-on effects, has any detectable adverse effect on comparative productivity. An inspection of the data for *WDL* reveals why this should prove no surprise. In most industries the proportion of days lost through strikes is very small. Moreover, the industrial distribution of days lost is similar in the two countries. Therefore, *WDL* has little variance. For 1967/8 its sample mean is 1.001, and the range ±0.001 of this mean includes 61 per cent of the industries.

The comparative degree of unionisation, *UNION*, obtains mixed results. For 1967/8 its coefficient is negative and carries a t-statistic that varies between specifications from 1 to 2; in equations 3 and 4 of table 3.3 it is significant at 10 per cent in a one-tail but not a two-tail test. For 1967/8 it takes a significant negative coefficient in our overall most satisfactory equation (table 3.4, below). However, for 1977 the variable proved insignificant throughout. Whether we should read into this difference a substantive change or simply an unclear result is the interesting, but unanswerable, question.

As equation 3 shows, strike intensity (*STRIK*) is neither significant nor regular in sign. An inspection of the correlations between *STRIK* and other variables suggests a serious problem of multicollinearity, expected in the light of our ability to explain *STRIK*'s British and American components in the course of deriving the variable *BEL* (see table 3.2). The relationship with plant size is particularly interesting: we find in each country a positive relation between strike intensity and plant size; but there also exists a positive relation between *comparative* strike intensity and British plant size (0.625 for 1967/8, 0.437 for 1977). It would appear that, while large-plant industries are more strike-prone in both countries (thus confirming Prais, 1981, Chapter 7 and our extension in Chapter 2), this effect is more pronounced in Britain than in America. Still, our research design proves unable to distinguish the effects of frequent strikes from the context of the large plants in which they principally occur; just as with the managerial variables, we establish that 'trouble' lies in the large-plant sector, but we cannot impute it further to managerial capability, labour relations, or other factors.

Equation 4 includes *BEL*, our residual measure of the unobserved bellicosity of an industry's labour relations. For 1967/8 its coefficient is negative as expected and significant at the 10 per cent confidence level in equation 4 and in our final 'preferred' specification. However, for 1977 it turns around astonishingly and obtains a weakly significant positive coefficient.

The depth of perversity in this result provoked some reconsideration of the hypothesis as well as diagnostic investigations of the data. First, the climate of labour relations during the 1970s in Britain (and other industrial countries) changed markedly as labour sought to avert the real-wage loss

Table 3.3 *Test of hypotheses concerning determinants of* VPW, *1967/8 and 1977*[a]

Equation no.		Independent variables related to efficiency	R^2	F	$\bar{R}^2$
1	A	0.020^b RD + 0.055 MGR + 0.011 $MGRRDK$ + 0.105 $FOSK$ (2.19) (0.55) (0.25) (0.71)	0.580	8.76	0.655
	B	0.011 RD + 0.339 MGR + 0.265 $MGRRDK$ + 0.212 $FOSK$ (1.14) (0.24) (0.85) (0.16)	0.435	5.48	0.533
2	A	0.020^b RD (2.26)	0.587	10.45	0.650
	B	0.015^b RD (1.67)	0.448	6.80	0.525
3	A	-0.083 $UNION$ -0.281 $STRIK$ (1.20) (1.08)	0.564	8.87	0.636
	B	0.176 $UNION$ + 0.419 $STRIK$ (0.23) (1.52)	0.439	6.20	0.524
4	A	-0.111^c $UNION$ -0.377^c BEL (1.56) (1.56)	0.573	9.16	0.643
	B	0.034 $UNION$ + 0.433^{cc} BEL (0.45) (1.73)	0.444	6.30	0.528
5	A	-0.003 $SIZE$ -0.196 $SMAL$ + 0.062 VI (0.07) (0.90) (0.98)	0.553	7.96	0.633
	B	0.024 $SIZE$ + 0.128 $SMAL$ + 0.030 VI (0.71) (0.63) (0.57)	0.420	5.5	0.513
6	A	0.113^c $IMEX$ (1.61)	0.635	9.05	0.713
	B	0.135^b $IMEX$ (1.71)	0.463	7.06	0.512
7	A	0.125^b $IMEXK$ (2.31)	0.589	10.49	0.651
	B	0.127^a $IMEXK$ (2.44)	0.468	7.29	0.542

[a] Each equation also includes all variables contained in the neoclassical core model and listed in table 3.1, except that the 1977 equations also include *CAPK*. Because their coefficients and significance levels are relatively unaffected by changing specifications of the efficiency terms, except as noted in the text, they are omitted to conserve space. Equation 6 was estimated with a reduced sample (52 for 1967/8, 59 for 1977), due to unavailable United States observations.

Notes: Levels of statistical significance: where one-tail tests are appropriate, a = 1 per cent, b = 5 per cent, c = 10 per cent; where two tail tests are appropriate, aa = 1 per cent, bb = 5 per cent, cc = 10 per cent.

A = 1967/8: B = 1977.

that followed from the energy-price increase. The scope for defensive measures was surely greatest in the industries that were concentrated and capital-intensive, and where rents (or quasi-rents) might be appropriated through strikes and bargaining. Because these industries display high (unadjusted) labour productivity, it seems quite possible that 'residual bellicosity' in the 1970s possessed a component positively correlated with productivity. Examination of some correlations confirms this.[12] Furthermore, if we enter the concentration ratio for each country into the equations used to derive *BEL* (table 3.2), it is quite insignificant for 1967/8 but in

Table 3.4 *Preferred results, full model of determinants of* VPW, *1967/8 and 1977*

1967/8

$$\log VPW = -0.138 + 0.150^a \log CAP + 0.352^{aa} \log CHECAP - 0.145^{aa} \log ELCAP$$
$$\quad (1.12) \quad (4.25) \qquad\qquad (5.51) \qquad\qquad\qquad (3.34)$$
$$\quad -0.134^{aa} \log BMCAP - 0.055^{aa} \log TPK + 0.371^{aa} \log ELTP - 0.362^b PCF$$
$$\quad (2.78) \qquad\qquad (2.70) \qquad\qquad (4.40) \qquad\qquad (2.03)$$
$$\quad -1.148^a PART - 0.394^{cc} NOPS + 0.156^a ED - 0.396^c BEL - 0.133^b UNION$$
$$\quad (3.98) \qquad (1.86) \qquad\quad (3.96) \qquad (1.81) \qquad (2.05)$$
$$\quad +0.024^a RD + 0.160^a IMEXK$$
$$\quad (2.85) \qquad (3.15)$$
$$R^2 = 0.718;\ \bar{R}^2 = 0.651;\ F = 10.73$$

1977

$$\log VPW = -0.167 + 0.130^b \log CAP + 0.251^{aa} \log CHECAP - 0.114 \log ELCAP$$
$$\quad (1.08) \quad (2.31) \qquad\qquad (2.81) \qquad\qquad\qquad (1.11)$$
$$\quad -0.143 \log BMCAP + 0.092^a \log TP - 0.106^{aa} \log TPK + 0.047 \log ELTP$$
$$\quad (1.33) \qquad\qquad (4.58) \qquad\quad (4.56) \qquad\qquad (1.14)$$
$$\quad -0.176 PCF - 0.826^b PART + 0.099^a ED + 0.481^{bb} BEL + 0.018^b RD$$
$$\quad (0.82) \qquad (2.08) \qquad\quad (2.61) \qquad (2.07) \qquad\quad (2.10)$$
$$\quad +0.142^a IMEXK + 0.069^{bb} CAPK$$
$$\quad (2.83) \qquad\qquad (2.01)$$
$$R^2 = 0.586;\ \bar{R}^2 = 0.512;\ F = 7.98$$

Note: Where one-tail tests of significance are appropriate, a = 1 per cent, b = 5 per cent, c = 10 per cent; where two-tail tests are appropriate, aa = 1 per cent, bb = 5 per cent, cc = 10 per cent.

1977 obtains t-statistics of 1.23 for the United Kingdom and 2.48 for the United States. While this pattern supports the proposition that the content of *BEL* had fundamentally altered by 1977, we might still cling to the 1967/8 result, but only if *BEL* for 1967/8 inserted into the 1977 model (for those industries matched between the two years) gives results similar to those for 1967/8. That it does not: *BEL* for 1967/8 in the 1977 model obtains a positive coefficient with a t-statistic not a great deal smaller than that for the 1977 version of *BEL*. Thus, while we do believe that the 1970s brought major changes to the climate of industrial relations, we can claim no more than that the data weakly support the 'residual bellicosity' hypotheses for the late 1960s.[13]

Industrial organisation and competition

Although the core model (table 3.1) gave us strong conclusions about plant size, economies of scale, and the locus of Britain's productivity problems in large plants, the additional variables addressing industrial organisation and competition added only modest amounts of additional insight. *SIZE*, *SMAL*, C_5 and *VI* proved quite insignificant in all specifications for both of the two sample years. Equation 5 indicates a sample of the results.

Domestic producer concentration proved an equally insignificant influence on productivity when interacted with trade exposure (*COMP*).

However, trade exposure itself does prove to have an important influence. As equations 6 and 7 of table 3.3 show, *IMEX* takes the expected positive sign but is not very significant, but *IMEXK* (trade exposure for the British industry only) proves to be significant in both years. Apparently overall exposure to international trade has no substantial effect on American productivity; *IMEXS* entered into the model receives an insignificant coefficient. But in the British economy (smaller, closer to major trading partners, and with perhaps more of a tradition of 'soft' competition that could be upset by foreign rivals), exposure to trade seems to have been a significant force for bringing improvements in productivity.

A complete econometric specification

We have considered the hypothesised determinants of efficiency in three groups, which must now be assembled into a final specification. In fact there is not much interaction among these groups, in the sense that variables significant (or insignificant) in the incomplete equations reported in table 3.3 retain their status when the model is fully assembled. Table 3.4 presents our best explanation of *VPW* for each year; best in the sense that variables not required in the core model and making no contribution to explained variance have been dropped. The R^2 value corrected for degrees of freedom is 0.65 for 1967/8 and 0.51 for 1977. These values can both be regarded as quite high for cross-section models, especially in the light of the 'noise' that inevitably enters through the transnational matching of industries and the assembly of data from diverse sources.

We performed one more test to assess the comparative performance of the model in the two years. We estimated the models shown in table 3.4 for the 63 industries matched in both 1967/8 and 1977, in order to compare the fits attained by the model on a common set of industries. Although the 1967/8 equation obtains a superior fit in table 3.4, the value of $\bar{R}^2$ on the common sample for 1977 (0.463) is appreciably higher than that for 1967/8 (0.403). In that sense we can say that the model's performance did not deteriorate between the two years.

Then, using the same set of industries, we 'switched' the two endogenous variables, regressing *VPW* for 1977 on the data for 1967/8 and *VPW* for 1967/8 on the exogenous variables for 1977. This exercise had several purposes, one being to assess the intertemporal stability of the estimated relationships. That is, if the regressors shifted a great deal between the two years, the fit of the estimated relationship would deteriorate sharply due to the switch even if the behavioural relationships persisted largely unchanged (as table 3.4 suggests they did). The deterioration in fact is fairly modest. When *VPW* for 1977 is regressed on exogenous variables for 1967/8, $\bar{R}^2$ deteriorates from 0.463 to 0.408. The complementary switch yields a larger deterioration when *VPW* for 1967/8 is fitted to the 1977 data from 0.403 to

0.209. This exercise yields no readily quantifiable conclusion, but it does indicate (in conjunction with table 3.4) both a set of largely persistent relationships and a fairly stable set of exogenous variables.

SUMMARY

We have established an empirical procedure for studying comparative industrial productivity. It builds on an approach derived from production-function relationships, and its application to samples of matched British and American manufacturing industries for 1967/8 and 1977 gives good statistical results in its 'neoclassical core.' That is, comparative labour productivity is related to comparative capital intensity, production-unit scales, and differences in human capital in ways that satisfy our theoretical prior expectations and accord with previous empirical evidence. The procedure accommodates differences in the production-function coefficients between the two countries and between broad industrial sectors, and these also seem to persist in stable fashion between the two years.

The neoclassical core of the model yields our most striking result concerning the determinants of efficiency in British industry. Whereas the typical industry in the United States enjoys access to moderate scale economies when the size of its typical plant expands, a statistically significant offset indicates that the typical United Kingdom industry enjoys no scale economies at all. There being no reason why technology should differ between the two countries, this result indicates strongly that something is amiss with productivity in large British plants.

With differences in industries' inputs controlled, we turn to the substantive hypotheses about the determinants of relative efficiency. Research intensity makes its expected positive contribution. Contrary to expectation, we found no statistical evidence of managerial failure in terms of either poor productivity in management-intensive industries or deficient inputs of managerial personnel. However, we did find that managerial inputs in the United Kingdom are highly correlated with typical plant size, so we cannot reject the hypothesis that managerial failure lies behind the typical British industry's inability to capture the economies of scale.

Our evidence on labour relations as a source of impaired productivity is inconsistent between the two years studied. The statistical evidence that, at roughly a 10 per cent significance level, productivity in the late 1960s was negatively related to the incidence of union membership and to a variable indicating the residual bellicosity of an industry's labour relations. However, in 1977 neither effect was apparent, and at this stage in our study the effect of labour relations on productivity remains a question mark.

Although relative productivity is unaffected by competition (measured by producer concentration) in the domestic market, it does increase with the extent of a British industry's exposure to international trade (both export opportunities and import competition). The relative size of the domestic market does not have an evident productivity-raising effect (contrary to 'Verdoorn's Law'), so that the effect of openness to international influences must depend at least partly on the competitive force that they inject. The relationship of productivity to size and to international transactions involves two-directional causality, however, so these conclusions remain tentative until we incorporate relative productivity in a simultaneous-equations context (Chapter 4).

4

PRODUCTIVITY, PRICES, MARKET STRUCTURE, AND INTERNATIONAL TRADE

In Chapter 1 we argued that low productivity in Britain is a causal factor affecting the structure of the economy as well as its overall capacity to generate income. Labour is used in prodigal fashion, for example, partly because it is cheap. More important for our inter-industry investigation, differences among industries in relative productivity affect the structure of the economy. Sectors with relative productivity disadvantages must charge high relative prices to cover their costs, curtailing demand and thereby reducing their scales of operation below what would otherwise prevail. Insofar as they face close international competition, their relative prices cannot be raised above those prevailing in the world market, and their outputs are further curtailed to levels such that the industry's long-run marginal cost can be covered at world prices.

RELATIVE PRODUCTIVITY AS CAUSE AND EFFECT

These general predictions about markets' adjustments to constraints on productivity have important implications for our statistical procedure. They identify forms of simultaneous-equations bias in the model estimated in Chapter 3 such that relative productivity (VPW) is expected to influence some of the variables that were employed as its determinants. This two-way causation generates correlations between the variables determining VPW and the error term in the VPW equation, the essential source of simultaneous-equations bias. Specifically, this bias operates along these channels:

1. Relative productivity is closely related to the fundamental determinants of patterns of international trade. Indeed, the classic concept of comparative advantage in its simplest form asserts that industries blessed with high relative productivity are likely to be prominent among a nation's exporters, while those with relative productivity disadvantages face extensive import competition. In our model, that relationship implies a reverse causality running from productivity to trade performance.[1] The measures of imports and exports that appear among the determinants of VPW are therefore not exogenous.

2. If the economy were closed to international trade, relative productivity would still influence industries' scales of operation, because a high

relative price (necessary to cover an inefficient sector's costs) curtails the quantity demanded. The size of the market ($SIZE$) therefore is not fully exogenous. Although that variable proved quite insignificant in Chapter 3, its failure could be the result of simultaneous-equations bias.

3. An important variable in our model, both conceptually and empirically, is typical plant size (TP and TPK). Although economists' 'favourite' set of assumptions makes the plant sizes chosen by entrepreneurs independent of the sizes of the markets that they serve, abundant empirical evidence asserts that a positive relation between plant size and market size is a pervasive (and analytically defensible) fact of industrial life. Therefore, relative productivity is expected to affect plant size, via relative prices and market size, so that TP and TPK are potentially endogenous variables.

4. Seller concentration is a variable that may affect VPW but also depend on it. Concentration, however measured, is a summary statistic describing some aspects of the number and size distribution of producer firms present in an industry. As such, it is closely related to typical plant size; indeed, we can write the standard n-firm concentration ratio as an identity depending on market size, typical plant size, the dispersion of plants' sizes, and the extent of multiplant operation. Therefore, C_5 depends on VPW via TP and its determinants. C_5 also depends on VPW via market size and the industry's export opportunities and competing imports.

Because of these strong *a priori* reasons for suspecting simultaneity, we now embed our model of VPW in a simultaneous-equations system to be estimated by the technique of instrumental variables. The substantive merit of this expansion lies in the opportunity to test various causal influences wielded by the relative productivity levels of Britain's manufacturing industries. The statistical need for this expansion stems from the simultaneous-equations bias that may afflict the coefficients of the models estimated in Chapter 3. The magnitudes and indeed the significance of important coefficients may change when these simultaneous relationships are allowed for.

A SIMULTANEOUS MODEL — GENERAL STRUCTURE

The list of simultaneous relationships presented above indicates the appropriate general shape of the expanded model. Clearly, $SIZE$ (relative market size) and C_5 (difference in producer concentration) should be included along with VPW as endogenous variables. So should some measures of exposure to international trade and typical plant size, but their exact forms require some consideration.

Plant size surfaces in our ordinary least squares model embodied in two variables; comparative UK/US plant size and absolute United Kingdom plant size. Should both be treated as endogenous? Clearly, much of the variance among industries in the typical plant's absolute scale is driven by technological factors; whether absolute plant scale is measured from British (as it is) or American data, its variance will largely reflect differences in technology. *TP*, however, was constructed in order to remove just this technological influence via the United States plant-size measure, thereby revealing the economic forces determining British plant sizes. On this argument, it is clearly *TP* that should be treated as endogenous while *TPK* is taken as exogenous.

The other problem concerns the treatment of exports and imports in the expanded model, and it turns more on data limitations than on conceptual issues. In the research underlying Chapter 3 we combined an industry's participation in exports and its exposure to import competition into a single variable, designated *IMEX* in its relative form. Our decision to couple those two influences was partly tactical and designed to minimise the degree to which simultaneous-equations bias affected our ordinary least squares estimates. That constraint need no longer be honoured as we construct the simultaneous-equations system. However, a data problem also influences our options. That is the impossibility of matching trade flows to domestic production for the American branches of some of our matched industries; this costs significant numbers of degrees of freedom when the trade variables are expressed in the form of UK/US relatives. That fact, coupled with the significant influence of total trade exposure in its British (*IMEXK*) but not its relative form (found in Chapter 3), leaves up in the air the question of how to enter trade exposure into the expanded model. We employ *IMEXK* as an endogenous variable in our principal version of the expanded model, but we do consider whether the conclusions change if another specification is substituted.

These considerations suggest a simultaneous model of the form:

$$VPW = f_1 \, (TP, \, IMEXK, \, SIZE, \, C_5, \, X_1) \tag{1}$$
$$TP = f_2 \, (SIZE, \, X_2) \tag{2}$$
$$SIZE = f_3 \, (PRICE, \, X_3) \tag{3}$$
$$IMEXK = f_4 \, (PRICE, \, TP, \, X_4) \tag{4}$$
$$C_5 = f_5 \, (TP, \, IMEXK, \, SIZE, \, X_5) \tag{5}$$

with *PRICE* related to *VPW* by the following identity:

$$PRICE \equiv VPW^{-1} * PROFIT^{-1} * WAGE$$

where *WAGE* indicates comparative earnings per employee. This identity implies a sixth endogenous variable, *PROFIT*, which is defined as:

PROFIT = comparative labour share of value added

We hypothesize the following model for determining it:

$$PROFIT = f_6 \, (TP, \, IMEXK, \, C_5, \, X_6) \tag{6}$$

In these equations the X_i ($i = 1 \ldots 6$) refer to the six vectors of exogenous variables included in the equations. The elements in these vectors need not be mutually exclusive.

We now provide a brief discussion of each of these additional variables and the rationales for the particular specifications that we employ. *TP*, besides depending on industry size (*SIZE*), should be affected by several exogenous variables. One is relative capital intensity (*CAP*). *TP* is measured in labour units, so that increased capital intensity involves a substitution away from labour and thus a reduction in the measured size of a plant accounting for any given share of output in the market. It should also depend on the extent to which non-production activities are performed alongside physical production, which is reflected in the relative proportion of non-production workers (*NOPS*). Evidence reviewed in Chapter 3 suggested that countries may differ in factors governing the viability of small plants, and so we include the difference in the prevalence of plants employing fewer than 50 workers (*SMAL*) as a regressor. Finally, the British and American economies may differ in plant-size distributions because of the large geographical area of the United States, which can lead to shrunken plant sizes in industries that are regionalised by high transportation costs. We assume that spatial constraints on plant sizes are significantly weaker in Britain. The variable that we employ is

REGS = average distance shipped within the United States for output classified to the United States industry.

The smaller is *REGS*, the more are American plant sizes attenuated by shipping costs, and the greater should be *TP*. In summary, *TP* should be negatively related to *SMAL*, *CAP*, and *REGS* but positively related to *SIZE* and *NOPS*.

Explanation of the sizes of industries is hardly a speciality of economic analysis, and the chief interest in the determinants of *SIZE* lies in its dependence on *PRICE*.[2] To complete the model as best we could, we incorporated two other variables. One is the difference between ratios of research and development expenditures to sales in the United Kingdom and the United States (*RD*).[3] The exploitation of the fruits of its research should enlarge an industry's sales and thus cause *RD* to wield a positive influence on *SIZE*. Similarly, we employ the variable

AD = advertising–sales ratio of the United Kingdom industry minus that for its United States counterpart.

Several studies have confirmed the hypothesis that an industry's total sales increase with the level of its advertising outlays, implying that *SIZE* should increase with *AD*.

The variable *IMEXK* offers a richer opportunity for economic analysis. Even though in this version of the system we do not disaggregate the variable into its export and import components, thereby invoking the familiar literature on the empirical determinants of comparative advantage, we can nonetheless explore some interesting issues concerning the factors that may explain an industry's total exposure to international trade. Nonetheless, some regressors may be deemed to influence imports or exports, but not both. To set the scene for specifying *IMEXK*, we recall the conclusion from Chapter 3 that the trade exposure of American industries does not seem to affect relative productivity; therefore, in specifying the determinants of *IMEXK*, we assume that *IMEXS* is effectively a constant, so that it is reasonable to regard exogenous variables in ratio or difference form as determining the absolute value of the British trade-exposure ratio.

Several endogenous variables should affect *IMEXK*. Although plant size might normally be regarded as a determinate rather than a determinant of trade exposure, the results of Chapter 3 do suggest a special influence for *TP* in the British context. We found that the various sources of the United Kingdom's productivity disadvantage coalesce around large-scale plants, so that industries with relatively large plant sizes in Britain should suffer systematic disadvantages in export markets. It is not clear that they have been similarly susceptible to import competition expecially in the light of the aid forthcoming from public policy in the 1970s. *TP*'s influence therefore should be negative.

Finally, the influence of *PRICE* on *IMEXK* is unclear because of the opposite-sign effects expected on imports and exports. If the principal exporting industries are able to charge different prices to domestic and foreign buyers, only the effect on imports would operate, and a positive sign would be expected. On the other hand, Britain's small size in the world market may suffice to make exports substantially more sensitive to relative prices than are imports, in which case *PRICE* would take a negative sign.

Of the exogenous variables that may affect *IMEXK*, some can be given definite sign predictions. Some evidence indicates that extensive intra-industry trade (that is, high levels of both exports and imports) occurs in industries subject to high levels of product differentiation and technical complexity (Caves, 1981). That would imply positive influences on trade exposure for research intensity (*RD*), skill intensity (*ED*), management intensity (*MGR*), advertising intensity (*AD*), and the relative importance of non-production workers (*NOPS*). It should decrease with the degree to which a manufacturing industry utilises raw materials among its inputs, because the localisation of production of most raw materials tends to make a processing industry either import competing or an exporter but not both. The variable that we employ is based on the American input–output structure, taken as a convenient proxy for the industry's universal structure:

RAW = sum of input coefficients from primary sectors for the United
        States counterpart industry.

The bellicosity of labour relations in the United Kingdom should serve as a deterrent to effective competition on export markets, although it may also increase imports (and thereby have an indeterminate net effect on *IMEXK*). Finally, evidence on the locational and sourcing behaviour of multinational enterprises suggests that their presence in Britain (*FOSK*) should increase an industry's trade exposure.[4] In summary, *IMEXK* should be positively related to *ED, RD, NOPS, AD, MGR*, and *FOSK*. It should be negatively related to *TP, RAW*, and *BEL*, and its relation to *PRICE* secures no sign prediction.

The difference between United Kingdom and United States producer concentration (C_5) should increase with relative plant size (*TP*) because of the identity relationship between them. It should similarly decrease with market size (*SIZE*). The effect of trade exposure is indeterminate;[5] because its expected effects are second-order and operate differently for exports and imports, we omitted it from the model. Among exogenous variables, it should increase with capital intensity (*CAP*), research intensity (*RD*), and advertising intensity (*AD*) because of the relation that each variable may exhibit to barriers to entry. It should be negatively related to the (inverse) indicator of regional submarkets in the United States (*REGS*), because American producer concentration measured at the national level should increase with *REGS*, and differential concentration (C_5) should therefore decrease. Similarly, the relative number of plants per firm among the largest five companies (*PF*) should be negatively related to *TP* as an indicator of unobserved incentives for the leaders to disperse their production facilities. In summary, positive signs are predicted for *TP, CAP, RD*, and *AD*, negative signs for *SIZE, PF*, and *REGS*.

The last equation in the model determines the measure of gross profitability (*PROFIT*) that appears in the identity that connects *PRICE* and *VPW*. It is defined empirically as

PROFIT = comparative labour share of valued added.

As an inverse measure of relative price–cost margins, it should be negatively related to C_5 and positively related to trade exposure (*IMEXK*). Negative relations are expected for the entry-barrier variables *TP, CAP, RD*, and *AD*. *REGS* indicates inversely the understatement of effective concentration in the United States due to regional submarkets. Therefore, it should be negatively related to the profit rate of the American industry and also to *PROFIT* (itself an inverse measure of UK/US profitability).

STATISTICAL RESULTS

Table 4.1 contains the results of estimating this system on the data for 1977 including, for comparison, a model of the determinants of *VPW* estimated by ordinary least squares (equation 1). When this model is estimated by means of instrumental variables (equation 2), several interesting results are

Table 4.1. *Estimation of simultaneous system of relations, 1977*

Ordinary least squares

(1) $\log VPW = -0.083 + -0.106^a \log TP + 0.032 \log SIZE + 0.145^a \log IMEXK$
$\quad\quad\quad\quad (0.53) \quad\ (5.06) \quad\quad\quad\quad (1.06) \quad\quad\quad\quad (2.87)$
$\quad\quad\quad -0.032 \log C_5 + 0.116^b \log CAP + 0.077^b \log CAPK + 0.262^{aa} \log CHECAP$
$\quad\quad\quad\ (0.63) \quad\quad (2.06) \quad\quad\quad\quad (2.19) \quad\quad\quad\quad\quad (2.91)$
$\quad\quad\quad -0.069 \log ELCAP - 0.124 \log BMCAP - 0.116^{aa} \log TPK - 0.236\ PCF$
$\quad\quad\quad\ (0.75) \quad\quad\quad\quad (1.15) \quad\quad\quad\quad (5.15) \quad\quad\quad\quad (1.05)$
$\quad\quad\quad -0.786^b\ PART + 0.090^b\ ED + 0.021^b\ RD + 0.559^{bb}\ BEL$
$\quad\quad\quad\ (1.95) \quad\quad\quad\quad (2.32) \quad\quad (2.38) \quad\quad (2.26)$

$R^2 = 0.588; \bar{R}^2 = 0.509$

Instrumental variables

(2) $\log VPW = 0.045 + 0.144^a \log TP + 0.088^c \log SIZE + 0.142^c \log IMEXK$
$\quad\quad\quad\quad (0.24) \quad (4.95) \quad\quad\quad\quad (1.57) \quad\quad\quad\quad (1.57)$
$\quad\quad\quad -0.181^{cc} \log C_5 + 0.103^c \log CAP + 0.099^{bb} \log CAPK + 0.295^{aa} \log CHECAP$
$\quad\quad\quad\ (1.77) \quad\quad\quad (1.54) \quad\quad\quad\quad (2.28) \quad\quad\quad\quad\quad (2.93)$
$\quad\quad\quad -0.107 \log ELCAP - 0.089 \log BMCAP - 0.127^{aa} \log TPK - 0.479^b\ PCF$
$\quad\quad\quad\ (1.05) \quad\quad\quad\quad (0.74) \quad\quad\quad\quad (4.84) \quad\quad\quad\quad (1.80)$
$\quad\quad\quad -0.676^c\ PART + 0.071^c\ ED + 0.028^a\ RD + 0.874^{aa}\ BEL$
$\quad\quad\quad\ (1.43) \quad\quad\quad\quad (1.55) \quad\quad (2.69) \quad\quad (2.81)$

(3) $\log TP = 0.493 + 0.453^b \log SIZE - 0.045^a \log SMAL - 0.908^a \log CAP$
$\quad\quad\quad\ (1.06) \quad (2.02) \quad\quad\quad\quad (5.90) \quad\quad\quad\quad (3.07)$

(4) $\log SIZE = -3.12^{aa} - 2.74^b \log PRICE + 0.960\ RD + 0.167\ AD + \text{sector dummies}$
$\quad\quad\quad\quad (3.80) \quad (1.80) \quad\quad\quad\quad (0.29) \quad\quad\ (0.19)$

(5) $IMEXK = -1.385^{bb} - 0.110^{bb} \log TP - 2.58^{bb} \log PRICE - 0.244^{aa}\ ED + 0.004\ RD$
$\quad\quad\quad\quad (2.03) \quad\ (2.47) \quad\quad\quad\quad (2.35) \quad\quad\quad\quad (2.71) \quad\quad\ (0.24)$
$\quad\quad\quad + 1.34^{bb}\ NOPS + 0.026\ ADC - 0.027\ RAW + 2.749\ MGR + 0.048^b\ FOSK$
$\quad\quad\quad\ (2.00) \quad\quad\quad (0.55) \quad\quad\quad (0.59) \quad\quad\quad (1.12) \quad\quad\ (1.75)$

(6) $\log C_5 = 0.308 + 0.173^a \log TP - 0.131 \log SIZE + 0.041^{bb}\ RD - 0.030^{cc} \log REGS$
$\quad\quad\quad\ (1.54) \quad (3.34) \quad\quad\quad\quad (1.10) \quad\quad\quad\quad (2.33) \quad\quad\quad\quad (1.72)$
$\quad\quad\quad + 0.645\ PF + 0.028\ ADC + 0.013\ KBARR$
$\quad\quad\quad\ (0.70) \quad\quad (0.63) \quad\quad\ (0.19)$

(7) $\log PROFIT = -0.435 - 0.102^b\ CAP - 0.012^c\ RD + 0.080 \log REGS - 0.329^c\ IMKD$
$\quad\quad\quad\quad\ (1.50) \quad (2.07) \quad\quad\quad (1.37) \quad\quad\ (1.63) \quad\quad\quad\quad (1.35)$
$\quad\quad\quad + 0.438^c\ EXKD - 0.021\ ADC - 0.035^c\ TP$
$\quad\quad\quad\ (1.47) \quad\quad\quad\quad (0.99) \quad\quad\ (1.57)$

Note: Levels of statistical significance: where one-tail tests are appropriate, a = 1 per cent, b = 5 per cent, c = 10 per cent; where two-tail tests are appropriate, aa = 1 per cent, bb = 5 per cent, cc = 10 per cent.

obtained. Of the variables endogenous to the system, the coefficients of *TP* and *IMEXK* remain statistically significant as before, and the coefficient of *TP* increased somewhat. The coefficient of *SIZE* becomes significant at the 6 per cent level (one-tail test), and the coefficient of the difference in concentration (*C5*) is negative and significant at the 10 per cent level in a two-tail test. Although the confidence with which we reject the null hypothesis could be greater, the coefficient is large: a doubling of a British industry's concentration would depress its relative productivity by 18 per cent. Thus, taking account of the simultaneity in the system brings confirmation to two hypotheses about system-endogenous variables where it was lacking in the ordinary least squares results. The significance of *SIZE*, when *TP*'s dependence on *SIZE* is controlled, is a particularly revealing indicator of the channel through which productivity is influenced by exogenous factors. Of the possible mechanisms at work, recent research on productivity in Canada (Baldwin and Gorecki, 1983; Harris, 1984) inclines us to emphasise the gains in the forms of longer-run lengths and greater specialisation within plants that are facilitated in larger markets. However, economies of multiplant operation (Scherer *et al.*, 1975) probably also play some part.

The exogenous variables in equation (2) exhibit few important changes from the ordinary least squares results (equation 1). The significance of the difference in female proportions of the workforce (*PCF*) is increased, whilst that of the differences in schooling (*ED*) and in proportions of part-time workers (*PART*) is reduced. And one must glumly note that the perversely signed coefficient of *BEL* grows substantially larger.

The other equations of the extended model reveal some results that are interesting for their own sakes. Typical plant size (equation 3) increases with market size, as expected, and its coefficient indicates about the same elasticity that has been found in other studies. Also, *TP* decreases with the size of the population of absolutely small plants. Thus, the behavioural forces (whatever they may be) that affect the survival of small-plant fringes do show significant variation among these matched manufacturing industries.[6] *TP* shows the expected and significant negative relation to relative capital intensity (*CAP*).

The equation for *SIZE* confirms the one hypothesis critical to the extended model: that *SIZE* decreases with *PRICE*. The signs of the coefficients of *RD* and *AD* are as expected, but neither coefficient is significant. The equation as estimated also included a series of sector dummy intercepts (not shown), but none of them proved significant.

Trade exposure (equation 5) does decrease with typical plant size, as we expected given the status of large plants as the confluence of Britain's productivity problems. It decreases significantly with *PRICE* (two-tail test), a pattern that we suggested is consistent with exports being more sensitive than imports to differentiated British goods being over- or under-priced on the world market. The hypotheses about intra-industry trade and product differentiation find confirmation only in the significant positive coefficient of *NOPS*; the signs of *ADC*,[7] *RD*, and *MGR* are correct, but those of *ED* and *RD* are not. The expected positive influence of the prevalence of foreign investment in British industries (*FOSK*) is confirmed. The expected negative coefficient of *RAW* is not significant.

Differential seller concentration (equation 6) increases with typical plant size and decreases with relative market size (although the latter coefficient is not statistically significant). The absolute magnitudes of these two coefficients are approximately equal, suggesting that concentration in effect depends on market size measured in units of typical plant size. Differential concentration is positively related to differential research intensity, consistent with the model of Nelson and Winter (1978). However, differential values of the conventional entry-barrier variables are not significant, even after they are amended to match standard statistical proxies for barriers to entry.[8] This negative result may reflect the relatively minimal variation of the structural determinants of concentration between matched industries in large industrial countries (drawing as they do on common technologies of production and distribution). With these variables controlled, differential concentration does decrease with the inverse measure of regional fragmentation in the United States (*REGS*).

The equation (7) for *PROFIT* (the complement of the profits–value-added ratio) excludes relative concentration but includes the entry-barrier variables that should both determine concentration and affect profitability directly. *CAP*'s coefficient is significant (as a control for the capital intensity of production processes). The coefficients of *RD* and *TP* are correctly signed and weakly significant. The influence of international trade is handled by separating *IMEXK* into its import and export components and multiplying each by a dummy that equals one for industries in which producer concentration in the United Kingdom is high, zero otherwise. The resulting variables, *IMKD* and *EXKD*, both take appropriate signs but are only weakly significant. Of the remaining variables, the coefficient of *ADC* is correctly signed but that of *REGS* is not.

Effect of changes in specification of extended model

For reasons explained above, the lack of an unambiguously best way to specify import competition and export participation in the model led us to estimate several versions of the extended model. We dismantled *IMEXK* into its components, *IMK* and *EXK*, estimating separate equations for them specified like the equation for *IMEXK* in table 4.1. Then we substituted comparative trade variables *IM* and *EX* for *IMK* and *EXK*, obtaining thereby the theoretically preferred specification but suffering a large loss in degrees of freedom.

Table 4.2 reports the results for the determinants of *VPW*. Equation 1 reproduces for comparison equation 2, the instrumental-variables equation for *VPW* from table 4.1. When *IMEXK* is partitioned into its imports and exports components, we obtain equation 2 in table 4.2. It reveals that the disciplining effect of trade exposure on productivity comes entirely through the imports side. The significance of the capital-intensity variables is reduced, but other changes in the estimated determinants of *VPW* are

Table 4.2. *Determinants of* VPW *estimated by method of instrumental variables, with alternative specifications of imports and exports, 1977*

(1) $\log VPW =$ $0.045 + 0.144^{a} \log TP + 0.088 \log SIZE + 0.142^{c} \log IMEXK$
         (0.24) (4.59) (1.57) (1.57)
         $-0.181^{cc} \log C_5 + 0.103^{c} \log CAP + 0.099^{b} \log CAPK + 0.295^{aa} \log CHECAP$
         (1.77) (1.54) (2.28) (2.93)
         $-0.107 \log ELCAP - 0.089 \log BMCAP - 0.127^{aa} \log TPK - 0.479^{b} PCF$
         (1.05) (0.74) (4.84) (1.80)
         $-0.676^{c} PART + 0.071^{c} ED + 0.028^{a} RD + 0.874^{bb} BEL$
         (1.43) (1.55) (2.69) (2.81)

(2) $\log VPW =$ $0.155 + 0.152^{a} \log TP + 0.110^{b} \log SIZE + 0.552^{a} \log IMK - 0.168 \log EXK$
         (0.78) (4.74) (1.89) (2.35) (0.90)
         $-0.156 \log C_5 + 0.080 \log CAP + 0.073 \log CAPK + 0.235^{b} \log CHECAP$
         (1.50) (1.09) (1.59) (2.20)
         $-0.126 \log ELCAP - 0.127 \log BMCAP - 0.137^{aa} \log TPK - 0.512^{b} PCF$
         (1.22) (1.02) (5.03) (1.89)
         $-0.776^{c} PART + 0.055 ED + 0.023^{b} RD + 0.766^{bb} BEL$
         (1.61) (1.16) (2.16) (2.40)

(3) EXK $= -1.066 - 0.054^{c} \log TP + 0.051 \log C_5 - 1.85^{b} \log PRICE - 0.161^{bb} ED$
         (2.14) (1.40) (0.36) (2.31) (2.42)
         $-0.036 RD + 0.957^{b} NOPS + 0.015 AD - 0.005 RAW + 1.429 MGR + 0.027^{c} FOSK$
         (0.24) (2.04) (0.50) (0.16) (1.80) (1.29)

(4) IMK $= -0.221 - 0.067^{a} \log TP + 0.030 \log C_5 - 0.552 \log PRICE - 0.069 ED$
         (0.67) (2.58) (0.32) (1.03) (1.57)
         $+0.034 RD + 0.298 NOPS + 0.010 AD - 0.016 RAW - 1.22 MGR + 0.025^{c} FOSK$
         (0.35) (0.95) (0.52) (0.73) (1.02) (1.79)

Note: Levels of statistical significance: where one-tail tests are appropriate, a = 1 per cent, b = 5 per cent, c = 10 per cent; where two-tail tests are appropriate, aa = 1 per cent, bb = 5 per cent, cc = 10 per cent.

insubstantial. In this system the equations for TP and $SIZE$ are unchanged from those in table 4.1 (because they do not contain $IMEXK$), and the changes in the equations for C_5 and $PROFIT$ are uninteresting and hence not reported. We do include in table 4.2 the instrumental-variables equations for the determinants of EXK and IMK. Both trade measures depend negatively on TP, as we expected, but contrary to our prediction that negative influence on imports is stronger and more significant than the negative influence on exports. The economic mechanism at work here must therefore be regarded as somewhat unsettled. $PRICE$ does wield the expected significant negative influence on exports, but not the predicted positive influence on imports.[9]

As we predicted from consideration of intra-industry trade, both IMK and EXK increase with the extent of non-production workers and foreign investment, although $FOSK$'s significance level is weak, and $NOPS$ is significant only for EXK.

In the third extended system that we estimated, using IM and EX, the

Table 4.3. *Determinants of* VPW *estimated by method of instrumental variables, 1967/8, with alternative specifications of imports and exports*

Ordinary least squares

$$\log VPW = -0.025 + 0.046^c \log TP + 0.028 \log SIZE + 0.196^a EXK + 0.154 IMK$$
$$\quad\;\; (0.24) \quad (1.53) \qquad\quad (1.01) \qquad\qquad (2.77) \qquad\quad (1.14)$$
$$\quad + 0.142^a \log CAP + 0.345^{aa} \log CHECAP - 0.156^{aa} \log ELCAP - 0.141^{aa} BMCAP$$
$$\quad\;\; (4.07) \qquad\qquad (5.28) \qquad\qquad\quad (3.50) \qquad\qquad\quad (2.78)$$
$$\quad - 0.068^{aa} \log TPK + 0.317^{aa} \log ELTP - 0.359^b PCF - 1.15^a PART$$
$$\quad\;\; (3.11) \qquad\qquad (3.52) \qquad\qquad (2.02) \qquad (3.96)$$
$$\quad - 0.358^b NOPS + 0.154^a ED - 0.250 BEL - 0.107^c UNION + 0.027^a RD$$
$$\quad\;\; (1.75) \qquad\quad (3.81) \qquad (1.18) \qquad (1.64) \qquad\quad (3.11)$$

$\bar{R}^2 = 0.653$

Instrumental variables

$$\log VPW = \;\; 0.022 + 0.068^b \log TP + 0.058 \log SIZE + 0.350^a EXK + 0.293^c IMK$$
$$\quad\;\; (0.13) \quad (1.66) \qquad\quad (0.83) \qquad\qquad (3.03) \qquad\quad (1.34)$$
$$\quad + 0.140^a \log CAP + 0.331^{aa} \log CHECAP - 0.171^{aa} ELCAP - 0.163^{aa} \log BMCAP$$
$$\quad\;\; (3.57) \qquad\qquad (4.36) \qquad\qquad\quad (3.28) \qquad\qquad (2.97)$$
$$\quad - 0.081^{aa} \log TPK + 0.281^{aa} \log ELTP - 0.313^c PCF - 1.01^a PART$$
$$\quad\;\; (3.13) \qquad\qquad (2.67) \qquad\qquad (1.64) \qquad (3.09)$$
$$\quad - 0.391^{cc} NOPS + 0.153^a ED - 0.187 BEL - 0.111^c UNION + 0.032^a RD$$
$$\quad\;\; (1.73) \qquad\quad (3.26) \qquad (0.71) \qquad (1.54) \qquad\quad (3.38)$$

Note: Levels of statistical significance: where one-tail tests are appropriate, a = 1 per cent, b = 5 per cent, c = 10 per cent; where two-tail tests are appropriate, aa = 1 per cent, bb = 5 per cent, cc = 10 per cent.

number of observations shrank from the 94 available in tables 4.1 and 4.2 to only 59. This loss produced a general deterioration in the fit of the equation for *VPW*. The signs of all important variables remained the same, but significance levels showed the modest but pervasive declines that we would expect to result from the reduced degrees of freedom. As in table 4.2, import competition and not export opportunities proved to be the disciplining international force that increases productivity. The influences of *TP* and *TPK* remained significant as before, but those of *SIZE* and *C5* slipped below the threshold of significance.

The extended system estimated for 1967/8

We estimated a similar set of extended models for 1967/8, in order to assess the robustness of the results of applying instrumental-variables estimation and to seek any evidence that structural changes may have occurred over the decade. Table 4.3 closely parallels table 4.2, presenting an ordinary least squares model of the determinants of *VPW* with *IMK* and *EXK* included as regressors. The second equation in table 4.3 is its counterpart estimated by the method of instrumental variables. We also estimated a model (not shown) to explore the effects of employing *IM* and *EX* with an accordingly reduced number of observations (in this case, from 74 to 48).

A comparison of the ordinary least squares and instrumental-variables equations shows a pattern not differing greatly from the counterpart equations of table 4.2. C_5 is omitted as a regressor because missing observations cost additional degrees of freedom; when included, its coefficient is insignificant and leaves other conclusions unchanged. Again the coefficient and t-statistic for TP increase somewhat in the simultaneous model. The same is true for the coefficients of IMK and EXK, except that in the earlier period exports appeared to wield the strong discipline on productivity rather than imports (as in 1977). No obvious explanation for this shift comes to mind. The result for endogenous variable $SIZE$ is not as clear for 1967/8 as for 1977. In the instrumental-variables equations the significance of the labour-relations variables $UNION$ and BEL is reduced. The finding confirms the impression that our model has not succeeded in identifying an independent and robust influence of labour relations on relative productivity.

In other equations in the extended model for 1967/8 (not shown) the conclusions reached with the 1977 data set about the asymmetrical sensitivities of exports and imports to $PRICE$ are fully replicated for 1967/8. So is the positive association between trade flows and foreign investment in Britain, except that for 1967/8 the coefficient for exports is highly significant whilst that for imports only equals its standard error. The negative effect of the relative prevalence of small plants on TP was quite evident, but the negative association found for 1977 between CAP and TP did not appear in the earlier year. The influence of $PRICE$ on $SIZE$ was not significant for 1967/8. Overall, therefore, the results from the earlier year can be counted as generally similar to those for 1977 but somewhat weaker.

SUMMARY

Labour productivity may exert a causal influence on several variables that were tested in Chapter 3 as its own putative determinants, and so we constructed a simultaneous-equations model to assess the biases present in the model when estimated by ordinary least squares. The extended system includes as dependent variables relative typical plant size, relative market size, the British industry's exposure to international trade, relative producer concentration, and relative gross profit margins.

This procedure indeed placed among the significant determinants of relative productivity two variables that proved insignificant in Chapter 3. Productivity does appear to increase with market size (the relation known as Verdoorn's Law), and it decreases with relative producer concentration. Although the significance levels of both coefficients are shaky (10 per cent but not 5 per cent), the elasticities implied by their coefficients are substantial. Relative productivity remains negatively related to trade exposure, as before, with the effect turning out to come entirely through the imports side.

Some interesting results emerge from the other equations that fill out the model. Typical plant size is significantly responsive to market size and shows about the same elasticity found in other studies of this relationship (0.45), although we might have expected the depressed productivity of large British plants to have reduced this coefficient. Typical plant size, measured by employment, also significantly reflects capital–labour substitution.

Market size is negatively influenced by the industry's relative price, a result that holds no surprise but that is satisfying in the light of the influence of size as an explanatory variable in the equations for relative productivity and relative typical plant sizes. Relative price also depresses *IMEXK*, the overall extent of the United Kingdom industry's trade exposure, implying that the deterrent effect of a high price (due to low productivity, monopoly, or whatever) on export opportunities more than offsets its tendency to cede the home market to importers. This interpretation is confirmed when we unbundle the dependent variable trade exposure into its import and export components. Trade exposure increases with the extent of foreign investment in the United Kingdom industry, consistent with the complementary relationship between trade and foreign investment that has recently emerged in other studies; the relation holds at least weakly for both exports and imports when they are considered separately.

The equation for differential concentration produces results consistent with many cross-section studies of concentration in single countries. It decreases with relative market size expressed in units of typical plant size. It is not affected significantly by the relative values of entry-barrier variables, but that may be due to a minimal amount of variance in structural entry barriers between these two economies. Dynamically, differential concentration does increase with differential rates of spending on research and development. It also increases with the relative importance of foreign direct investment in the United Kingdom market.

The statistical results reported in detail in the chapter and summarised here are taken from the 1977 cross-section of data. When the same model is estimated on the 1967/8 cross-section, all important results remain as before with these exceptions: market size is not a significant determinant of relative productivity; concentration also loses its negative influence on relative productivity, perhaps due to missing observations for the earlier year; exports seem to wield a strong influence on relative productivity, whereas imports did in 1977. The puzzle concerning the labour-relations determinants of efficiency, left over from Chapter 3, remains unresolved: the correctly signed coefficients of union membership and residual bellicosity deteriorate somewhat in significance for 1967/8, and the perversely signed coefficient of bellicosity for 1977 grows somewhat larger.

5

RELATIVE PRODUCTIVITY IN LARGE PLANTS

A central finding of the study has been that productivity performance in the United Kingdom is especially inferior in industries whose plants are large. Although we have not established statistical evidence of managerial shortcomings or costs of antagonistic labour relations *after* controlling for typical plant sizes, ample evidence has emerged that these factors are all collinear. This finding agrees with a good deal of background evidence that was reviewed in Chapter 1.

With the productivity problem sited in large plants, we sought to adapt our research design to focus more sharply on the position of large plants in the United Kingdom. This can be done in a number of ways, and the one that we chose offers the convenience of a close affinity to our basic research design. We utilised the typical or median plant size that was identified as a variable in the neoclassical core model (Chapter 2) to calculate these measures of relative productivity (defined exactly as in *VPW*) for large and small plants:

$VPW1$ = relative labour productivity in plants larger than median plant size;

$VPW2$ = relative labour productivity in plants smaller than median plant size.

Median plant size of course differs from industry to industry. Thus, the approach is not designed to isolate the traits of plants larger and smaller than some common absolute size. Rather, it emphasises the comparative performance of the plants that are the largest (or smallest) in each industry. Given the well-established collinearity between plant sizes and firm sizes within industries, the approach dwells equally on large and small firms.

DESCRIPTIVE ANALYSIS

A descriptive analysis of our two cross-section samples (for 1967/8 and 1977) yields some interesting insights and affirms the fruitfulness of this approach. We can decompose VPW for industry i as follows:

$$VPW_i \equiv \{\frac{0.5(Y_1K)+0.5(Y_2K)}{0.5(Y_1S)+0.5(Y_2S)}\}_i \equiv VPW1_iw_i + VPW2_i(1-w_i)$$

where $VPW1_i = (Y_1K/Y_1S)_i$, the ratio of labour productivity in large British plants relative to the same in the United States. Similarly, $VPW2_i = Y_2K/Y_2S$.

Thus, the aggregate labour productivity ratio for a given industry is the weighted average of VPW_1 and VPW_2 with the weight defined as:

$$w_i = \{Y_1S/(Y_1S + Y_2S)\}_i = (1 + Y_2S/Y_1S)_i^{-1}$$

This expression indicates that VPW_1 is most important in industries for which Y_1S/Y_2S is high. That is the ratio of large to small-plant productivity in the American counterpart industry, and so we can interpret w as an indicator of the degree of scale advantage inherent in the industry.[1]

When we aggregate across the sample, we obtain:

$$\overline{VPW} = \bar{w}*\overline{VPW_1} + (1 - \bar{w})\overline{VPW_2} + \{\mathrm{cov}(VPW_1, w) - \mathrm{cov}\ (VPW_2, w)\}$$

where bars over variables denote sample means, and the covariance term appears because w_i varies among industries. Inserting the actual magnitudes for the 1967/8 sample, we find

$$0.4026 = (0.5195 \times 0.404) + (0.4805 \times 0.405) + (-0.0023 - 0.0036)$$

For 1977 the results are:

$$0.4110 = (0.5290 \times 0.404) + (0.4710 \times 0.418) + (-0.0021 - 0)$$

As can be seen, the average values of VPW, VPW_1, and VPW_2 are virtually identical in 1967/8: on average, the larger and smaller sectors of United Kingdom industries performed equally poorly against their United States counterparts, and in 1977 only a slight tendency was evident for the small-plant sectors to do relatively better than the large-plant sectors. But that similarity leaves open the possibility that something is wrong in absolutely large plants in Britain. Thus, whilst the two covariance terms in the preceding expression are small relative to the sample means, they do reflect significant negative correlations between w and VPW_1 ($r = -0.55$ for 1967/8, -0.46 for 1977) although not between w and VPW_2 ($r = -0.12$ for 1967/8, 0.01 for 1977). Thus, the larger sectors of United Kingdom industries perform significantly worse in industries characterised by more pronounced scale advantages.[2] In other words, it is in precisely those industries in which scale matters that large British plants perform poorest.[3]

We can decompose the variance of VPW and insert the sample magnitudes to obtain:

	1967/8	1977
$\bar{w}^2\mathrm{var}(VPW_1)$	0.27×0.01	0.28×0.012
$+ (1 - \bar{w})^2\mathrm{var}(VPW_2)$	$+0.23 \times 0.005$	0.22×0.009
$+ 2\bar{w}(1 - \bar{w})\mathrm{cov}(VPW_1, VPW_2)$	$+0.00254$	0.00294
$+ R$	$+0.0002$	0.0007
$= \mathrm{var}(VPW)$	$= 0.0066$	0.0089

Here the term R represents a messy expression reflecting the covariances of w and VPW_1 and VPW_2. The expression is easier to interpret if we express each of the component magnitudes as a proportion of the overall variance. In this form the variance of $VPW1$ for 1967/8 (41 per cent) is more than twice as important as that of $VPW2$ (17 per cent), although the fairly high sample correlation between $VPW1$ and $VPW2$ ($r = 0.718$) means that their covariance also contributes importantly (38 per cent). In other words, although poorly performing large and small plants tend to go hand-in-hand in the United Kingdom, there is far more variability in the relative performance of large plants. By 1977 the variance of VPW had increased about one-third. The variability of the relative productivity of the large plants (36 per cent) continued to dominate that contributed by small plants (22 per cent).

REGRESSION ANALYSES OF $VPW1$ AND $VPW2$

Our next task is to undertake separate regression analyses of $VPW1$ and $VPW2$. This manoeuvre permits a limited test of a key result that we have obtained so far: the conjunction of productivity-constraining factors in the large-plant sector. If the hypotheses that we have advanced concerning managerial factors, labour relations, or patterns of competition hold exclusively (or chiefly) for large plants, then their significance should be apparent (or more apparent) in the large-plant portions of our matched UK/US industries. This manoeuvre is akin statistically to a dodge around the problem of multicollinearity.

The exogenous variables to which we relate $VPW1$ and $VPW2$ are the same ones utilised in Chapter 3 for the matched industries as whole units. The reason for that is entirely pragmatic: the impossibility of constructing most of the exogenous variables for subsectors of industries from available data. Nonetheless, prior empirical research gives us bases for expecting that the variance of the exogenous variables will be due in different and somewhat predictable degrees to conditions in the large-plant sectors of the sampled industries. We shall draw on these bases for interpreting the regression results.

Table 5.1 shows the result of re-estimating the preferred equations for 1967/8 and 1977 (from table 3.4) with $VPW1$ and $VPW2$ as the dependent variables. For 1967/8 there is a striking difference between the unchanged explanatory power shown by the model when applied to the large-plant sectors and its appreciable weakening in the small-plant sectors. For 1977 this difference is much less marked, with the model's explanatory power only marginally stronger for the larger plants. Similarly, with three exceptions (PCF, $NOPS$, and $UNION$) the (absolute) magnitudes of the coefficients on the explanatory variables and the levels of significance are indeed enlarged for the large-plant sectors in 1967/8. For 1977 almost all the coefficients in the large-plant sector again exceed those for the whole

Table 5.1. *Determinants of* VPW, *large-plant and small-plant sectors of matched United Kingdom and United States manufacturing industries, 1967/8 and 1977*

Independent variable	1967/8		1977	
	Large plants	Small plants	Large plants	Small plants
Constant	0.071	−0.347^{aa}	−0.097	−0.593^{bb}
	(0.47)	(2.58)	(0.40)	(2.81)
log CAP	0.182^{a}	0.098^{a}	0.160^{b}	0.176^{b}
	(4.29)	(2.62)	(1.93)	(2.45)
log CAPK	—	—	0.076	0.089^{bb}
			(1.47)	(1.99)
log CHECAP	0.386^{aa}	0.315^{aa}	0.310^{aa}	0.441^{aa}
	(4.90)	(4.52)	(2.31)	(3.79)
log ELCAP	−0.265^{aa}	−0.106	−0.146	−0.181
	(3.03)	(1.38)	(0.98)	(1.39)
log BMCAP	−0.146^{bb}	−0.085	−0.187	−0.031
	(2.35)	(1.55)	(1.01)	(0.19)
log TP	—	—	0.115^{a}	0.023
			(3.88)	(0.89)
log TPK	−0.077^{aa}	−0.038^{bb}	−0.142^{aa}	−0.063^{bb}
	(3.02)	(1.66)	(4.05)	(2.07)
log ELTP	0.617^{aa}	0.224^{cc}	0.060	0.084
	(4.62)	(1.89)	(1.00)	(1.61)
PCF	−0.137	−0.544^{a}	0.071	−0.480^{c}
	(0.59)	(2.64)	(0.20)	(1.56)
PART	−1.451^{a}	−0.819^{a}	−0.741	−0.868^{c}
	(4.01)	(2.56)	(1.11)	(1.51)
NOPS	−0.323	−0.487^{bb}	0.064	0.291
	(1.23)	(2.09)	(0.16)	(0.84)
ED	0.180^{a}	0.113^{a}	0.111^{b}	0.074^{c}
	(3.68)	(2.61)	(1.89)	(1.46)
RD	0.041^{a}	0.014^{c}	0.018^{c}	0.022^{b}
	(3.52)	(1.32)	(1.41)	(2.04)
BEL	−0.582^{b}	−0.215	0.226	0.046
	(2.11)	(0.88)	(0.53)	(0.12)
UNION	−0.114	−0.108	—	—
	(1.40)	(1.50)		
IMEXK	0.209^{a}	0.136^{a}	0.133^{b}	0.077
	(3.27)	(2.42)	(1.79)	(1.19)
R^2	0.718	0.575	0.533	0.505
$\bar{R}^2$	0.646	0.467	0.433	0.399
F	10.01	5.32	5.33	4.76

Note: Levels of statistical significance: where one-tail tests are appropriate, a = 1 per cent, b = 5 per cent, c = 10 per cent; where two-tail tests are appropriate, aa = 1 per cent, bb = 5 per cent, cc = 10 per cent.

industries, but the differential in statistical significance is not substantial. Broadly speaking, most of the hypotheses are more strongly confirmed for large-plant sectors than they were for the industry aggregates, but the difference is more marked for the earlier year.

The most important difference between the small-plant and large-plant sector lies in the coefficient of TPK, much larger and more significant for the large-plant sector in both years. Thus we can sharpen our earlier conclusions on absolute plant size: the major cause of poorer United Kingdom performance in large-plant industries is the poorer performance of the larger plants in those industries. This is not quite so tautological as it might seem: the fact that a similarly significant effect is not found for TPK in the equation for $VPW2$ suggests that whatever lies behind TPK's effect is not *industry* but *large-plant* specific.

Also of substantial interest is the fate of the variable BEL, in the light of the puzzling behaviour exhibited in Chapter 3 by this measure of antagonism in labour relations. For 1967/8 its coefficient is larger and more significant in the large-plant sector than for the industry-wide aggregates, as we expect. For 1977 the perverse sign obtained in Chapter 3 persists, but the coefficient is not significant for either large or small plants. Although we can reach no strong conclusions on this variable, the evidence at hand does tend to keep the null hypothesis at bay for 1967/8.

The other regressors in table 5.1 merit a few remarks. In the case of RD it is well known that large firms (whether in a given industry or overall) are more likely than small ones to undertake formal R&D programmes. The coefficients of RD accordingly differ between large and small sectors for 1967/8, but the pattern fails for 1977. More consistently, large units employ more personnel with advanced educational qualifications (ED). The coefficients of $IMEXK$ are also larger in the large-plant sectors, as expected. Because of the higher fixed costs or scale economies in marketing abroad, large firms on average export larger proportions of their outputs than do their smaller competitors. Small firms are likely in any case to be price takers with respect to their larger rivals and therefore not directly affected by the overall degree of import competition faced by the industry. In each case the small-plant sectors should exhibit less variance in these variables, and what variance they do show will be inaccurately measured by the industry-wide exogenous variables.

Although its pattern differs between the years, we can inquire why the impact of CAP should be greater in larger plants in 1967/8. Two effects may be involved. First, for some industries, it may simply be incorrect to assume that large and small plants operate on the same production function, either because they utilise qualitatively different technologies or because they produce dissimilar outputs. Secondly, even if they are deemed to utilise the same production function, that function need not satisfy the assumption underlying our model that capital and labour are used in the same proportions no matter what scale of operation is elected. The empirical evidence indeed suggests that, within industries, capital intensity typically increases with plant size.[4] If so, the magnitude of the industrywide CAP understates absolute and relative capital intensity in the large-plant sector and correspondingly causes its effect (coefficient) to be overstated (and the opposite in the small-plant sector).

Finally, $NOPS$ and $UNION$ (in 1967/8) and PCF (both years) prove to be insignificant determinants of $VPW1$. We suspect the reasons for this are as follows. First, the incidence of female participation in large plants may be lower, especially in low-productivity occupations; if so, UK/US differences are more concentrated in the small-plant sectors, hence the increased significance of PCF in the equation for $VPW2$. Secondly, the occupations mix of $NOPS$ may differ between large and small plants, with large plants employing proportionally more technical and scientific staff but small plants proportionally more low-productivity manual non-operative staff. This is certainly consistent with the comfortably significant negative coefficient on $NOPS$ in the equation for $VPW2$, as well as with the results for RD and ED mentioned above. Third, the insignificance of $UNION$ in both equations echoes its insignificance for the industries as a whole. Here our lack of access to data for the industry subsectors may prove particularly costly; large plants are more commonly unionised than small ones, and large-plant sectors may in many cases be both fully unionised (that is, no inter-industry variance) and quite dissimilar to their small-plant industrial neighbours.

We experimented with specifications other than those shown in table 5.1, involving the other explanatory variables described in Chapter 3. In general the results are unremarkable, with the exception that in 1967/8 $STRIK$ (difference in number of strikes per plant) appears as a significant negative determinant of $VPW1$ but not $VPW2$. This is reflected indirectly in table 5.1 by a similar performance of the variable BEL. On the other hand, contrary to expectation, we found no evidence of a stronger or significant impact for the difference in management intensity, MGR. For 1977 we estimated the equations in table 5.1 by the method of instrumental variables, as in Chapter 4. The results differ very little from the OLS findings reported above. Apart from the expected slight deterioration in significance levels, the only substantial change is that $IMEXK$'s coefficients become quite insignificant.

SUMMARY

In order to pursue further our finding about the negative influence of British plant sizes on productivity in manufacturing, we disaggregated each sample industry in both countries into those plants larger and smaller than the one accounting for the median unit of output. Although British small-plant sectors on average perform about as poorly as large-plant sectors relative to their American counterparts, the United Kingdom large-plant sectors perform worse the greater are the scale economies apparently enjoyed by large plants in the United States. Correspondingly, the variability of British industries' relative performance in the large-plant sectors much exceeds the variability of their performance in the small-plant sectors. These findings amplify the negative influence on productivity of typical plant size reported in Chapters 3 and 4: large British plants fail to attain the productivity gains potentially available from scale economies and accordingly underperform their American counterparts more where scale economies are important; because the extent of scale economies varies from industry to industry, this also means that the productivity perform-ance of United Kingdom industries' large-plant sectors is more variable than that of their small-plant sectors.

We also re-estimated the principal models of relative productivity that emerged from Chapter 4 for the large-plant and small-plant sectors separately (using, however, only industry-wide variables as regressors). The models' explanatory powers are greater for the large-plant sectors, especially in 1967/8. The negative influence of United Kingdom labour relations is also more strongly evident for large plants in that year. However, the puzzling or insignificant findings on these variables for 1977 are mitigated only to the extent that the perverse-signed coefficient of the bellicosity measure is insignificant for the large-plant sector. The perform-ance of the variable measuring the absolute sizes of British plants affirms that British productivity falls short not just in these industries overall but specifically in their large-plant sectors. Thus, our dissection of industries into their large- and small-plant sectors does not solve the puzzle of how deficient large-plant performance may be related to managerial and labour-relations factors, but it does further confirm the malign influence of some set of factors concentrated in the large-plant sectors.

6

RELATIVE PRODUCTIVITY GROWTH

A natural progression leads us from an analysis of the relative productivity levels of British industries to their relative rates of productivity growth. Several contrasting models may be applied to the relation between an industry's productivity growth and the divergence of its productivity from the best level attainable. In the spirit of Gerschenkron's concept of relative backwardness, one can point to the cheap access to improved performance that is available to the producer who imitates his more advanced rival's best practices and avoids making the rival's mistakes. This hope glows brightest where productivity's shortfall is due to a lack of intangible assets (managerial practices, technological knowledge, and so forth) that can be taken up at low cost.

On the other hand, we suggested in Chapter 1 that some factors causing low productivity also tend to preserve or exacerbate a shortfall. Being productive in a world of rapid change demands an ability to alter course quickly when circumstances dictate. If low productivity results from social conditions and restrictive arrangements that preclude efficient production, they are very likely to shrivel the gains from responding to some external signal that best practice has changed.[1]

The descriptive statistics cited in Chapter 1 pointed in no clear direction as between these contrasting hypotheses. For the early postwar years (1950–62) Denison[2] found that overall residual productivity in Britain grew no faster than in the United States and slower than in other European countries. However, data for later periods have generally indicated that the United Kingdom was gaining a bit on the United States, although other industrial countries were gaining much faster. Internationally, the catch-up hypothesis vis-à-vis the United States productivity level works rather well for other industrial countries but not for Britain, as Martin's (1984) statistical investigation suggested.

If the catch-up hypothesis seems obviously inapplicable to the British economy as a whole, is it similarly inapplicable to individual British manufacturing industries? Or do those industries suffering low levels of productivity also tend to lag behind in productivity growth? Are differences among industries in relative productivity growth due to causal factors similar to the ones affecting relative productivity levels? An analysis of

Table 6.1. *Descriptive statistics, measures of growth in output per employee, total output, and employment, 61 matched British and American industries, 1968–77*

Variable	Sample mean	Sample standard deviation	Minimum	Maximum
Net output per employee				
VPWG	0.998	0.229	0.597	2.002
VPWGK	1.281	0.307	0.780	2.299
VPWGS	1.296	0.184	0.999	1.792
Employment				
LABG	0.919	0.195	0.457	1.466
LABGK	0.892	0.161	0.551	1.275
LABGS	0.989	0.166	0.697	1.520
Net output				
OUTG	0.910	0.250	0.457	1.656
OUTGK	1.154	0.388	0.518	2.505
OUTGS	1.278	0.269	0.792	1.925

relative productivity growth rates clearly complements our study of productivity levels.

SOME DESCRIPTIVE EVIDENCE

We developed a matched sample of 61 British and American industries for which productivity growth could be measured for the period 1968 to 1977. We did not simply align our 1967/8 and 1977 industry samples and calculate differences of productivity levels (and other variables), because we feared that the results would be seriously distorted by the imperfect procedure that was used to put relative nominal productivity levels into real terms. Instead we constructed a new sample of industries for which indices of output and input growth are available in both countries. The matched industries are listed in Appendix A.

The dependent variable is defined as

$$VPWG = VPWGK/VPWGS$$

where $VPWGK = (X_{1K}/X_{oK})/(L_{1K}/L_{oK})$ and $VPWGS = (X_{1S}/X_{oS})/(L_{1S}/L_{oS})$ and X refers to net output in constant prices and L to employment. The subscripts 1 and 0 refer to 1977 and 1968 respectively.

Table 6.1 reports the standard dimensions of these variables. It shows that average productivity growth in the sampled industries was almost identical in the two countries. The nine-year growth rate of 28.1 per cent in

Table 6.2. *Decomposition of mean and variance of logarithms of* VPWG

Variable	Productivity growth		Output growth		Labour growth		2xcov (output, labour growth)
Decomposition of mean log VPWG							
Comparative	−0.025	=	−0.131	−	(−0.106)		
UK	0.223	=	0.092	−	(−0.131)		
US	0.248	=	0.224	−	(−0.024)		
Decomposition of variance log VPWG							
Comparative	0.0455	=	0.0769	+	0.0449	−	0.0764
UK	0.0476	=	0.1027	+	0.0337	−	0.0888
US	0.0222	=	0.0431	+	0.0262	−	0.0471

the average industry is equivalent to an annual compound rate of just less than 3 per cent. However, within the sample there is considerably more inter-industry variability about the United Kingdom mean than about that for the United States counterpart industries. The American industries effectively avoided declines in productivity during the period, but none increased its productivity by more than 80 per cent, whereas the United Kingdom's range was much wider. That difference by itself gives no hint whether it is the British or the American dispersion that should be regarded as peculiar. However, Elliott and Hughes (1976, pp. 39, 65) observed the same difference as between Britain and Germany for the period 1954–72, suggesting that the high British variance may call for explanation.[3]

The correlation between *VPWGK* and *VPWGS* is 0.364, significant but not very high. Elliott and Hughes computed rank correlation coefficients from their UK/Germany data, securing 0.83 for labour productivity and 0.56 for total factor productivity.

Table 6.1 also includes the two components of labour-productivity growth, output growth and employment growth (*OUTG* and *LABG* respectively). A substantial difference between the two countries emerges. In the United Kingdom productivity growth was due in roughly equal proportions to output growth and employment contraction, while in the United States employment was typically maintained, and the increase in productivity reflected the increase in output.[4]

In statistical terms, the decomposition of *VPWG* into its constituent parts is more elegantly expressed in logarithmic terms (table 6.2). Thus, the slight shortfall of British productivity growth was reflected in slower output growth in the United Kingdom that was not quite counteracted by more rapid shedding of labour. The lines for the two countries separately show the same thing put another way: the growth in British productivity reflects output growth and labour shedding, with the latter more important; in the

Table 6.3. *Regressions of growth in net output per employee on growth of net output, 61 matched British and American industries, 1968–77[a]*

Dependent variable	Constant	Exogenous variable	$\bar{R}^2$
VPWGK	0.502 (0.065)	0.675 OUTGK (0.054)	0.722
VPWGS	0.688 (0.097)	0.467 OUTGS (0.074)	0.399
VPWG	0.432 (0.082)	0.620 OUTG (0.087)	0.453

[a] Standard errors appear in parentheses beneath the coefficients.

United States productivity growth was achieved with virtually no shedding of labour. The decomposition of the variances in the second part of table 6.2 shows that the variability of output growth accounts for the larger share of the variability of *VPWG*, although variations in employment growth are also important (as expected, these effects are dampened by the substantial positive correlation between the two constituents).

The evident difference in patterns of the growth of output and labour input between the two countries directs our attention at the outset to the association between productivity growth and output growth. This is familiarly referred to as Verdoorn's Law, although we pursue it here without the assumption often associated with it that productivity growth is caused by demand-based changes in total output. Table 6.3 presents simple regressions showing that the fit and slope coefficient are both much higher for the United Kingdom than for the United States. The British slope coefficient for 1968–77 is also noticeably higher than the values that Wragg and Robertson (1978, p. 21) reported for their earlier periods: 0.305 for 1954–63 and 0.509 for 1963–73. This suggests a steepening of the relationship in the United Kingdom[5] and, in the context of the preceding evidence, reinforces the hypothesis that the attainment of productivity gains may be particularly attenuated in industries that are experiencing little or no growth in output. Such a hypothesis is consistent with the result of Wenban-Smith (1981) that, from 1968–73 to 1973–9, British industries that suffered declines in productivity growth also suffered reductions in output growth, while industries with increasing rates of productivity growth were about equally divided between those with rising and falling rates of output growth. Unless some such explanation holds, the difference between the British and American patterns in table 6.3 seems to imply that British productivity would grow faster than American productivity at any common rate of output growth. Specifically, the British and American functions estimated in the table intersect at a value of $OUTG = 0.935$, implying that British productivity growth would be faster for any given growth rate that exceeds -6.5 per cent.

FRAMEWORK FOR ANALYSING COMPARATIVE RATES OF PRODUCTIVITY GROWTH

The model developed in Chapter 2 can be readily adapted to the analysis of comparative rates of productivity growth. Recall the basic form of the neoclassical core equation that was estimated in Chapter 3:

$$VPW_j = EFF_j * CAP_j^a * TP_j^{a+\beta-1} \text{ for all } j \tag{1}$$

We now express the growth of each variable between 1968 and 1977 as the ratio of its 1977 level to its 1968 level, denoting the transformed variables by adding the suffix G. Taking logarithms, we can write:

$$\log \dot{VPWG}_j = \log EFFG_j + a \log CAPG_j + (a+\beta-1) \log TPG_j \tag{2}$$

As before, we can add sector and country dummies to allow for variations in a and β. $CAPG$ can be measured directly from the variables used in the cross-section analyses for 1967/8 and 1977. $VPWG$, as we mentioned previously, is measured from index numbers of output and employment. In order to calculate TPG as accurately as possible, we change the definition of TP in the initial and terminal years from the median to the mean size of plants with more than 50 employees. That is because the median is measured inaccurately by interpolation, so that large errors could enter into TPG when it is calculated as a ratio.[6]

In table 6.4 equation (1) provides an estimate of the model set forth above. As before, we allow for differences between countries in the output elasticities a and β by entering the growth rates for the capital–labour ratio and typical plant size in the United States ($CAPSG$ and $TPSG$).[7] The equation implies rather different parameter values for the two countries:

	a	β	$a+\beta$
United Kingdom	0.393	0.698	1.091
United States	0.152	0.953	1.105

Consistent with the preceding evidence on productivity levels, labour is more productive in the United States, capital more productive in the United Kingdom. Returns to scale are somewhat stronger in the United States. The constant term here can be given a definite interpretation: absent any changes in factor inputs, the productivity differential shifts against the United Kingdom over the period by 15.4 per cent (linear approximation). Thus, the counterpart of our neoclassical core model gives results consistent with the analysis of productivity levels.

Table 6.4. *Determinants of relative productivity growth, 61 matched UK/US industries*

Independent variables	Equation (1)	Equation (2)	Equation (3)	Equation (4)	Equation (5)
Constant	−0.154[b] (1.90)	−0.058[b] (1.95)	−0.106[b] (2.21)	−0.212[a] (2.57)	−0.198[a] (2.39)
CAPG	0.393[aa] (2.67)	0.381[a] (2.81)	0.350[a] (2.54)	0.396[a] (2.80)	0.443[a] (3.05)
TPG	0.091 (1.19)	0.069[b] (2.24)	0.168[b] (2.23)	0.188[a] (2.55)	0.227[a] (2.86)
CAPSG	0.241[c] (1.31)			0.243[c] (1.40)	0.221 (1.27)
TPSG	−0.014 (0.09)				
CAPGD		−0.234 (1.10)	−0.210 (0.99)		
TPGD		−0.302[bb] (2.22)	−0.291[bb] (2.14)	−0.325[bb] (2.46)	−0.334[bb] (2.53)
EFF			−0.163 (1.27)	−0.158 (1.24)	−0.138 (1.08)
BMCAPG					−0.395 (1.29)
R^2	0.147	0.222	0.244	0.257	0.279
$\bar{R}^2$	0.085	0.166	0.175	0.190	0.199

Note: Where one-tail tests of significance are appropriate, a = 1 per cent; b = 5 per cent; c = 10 per cent. Where two-tail tests are appropriate, aa = 1 per cent; bb = 5 per cent; cc = 10 per cent.

Effect of declining employment

The descriptive evidence reviewed above suggests that productivity growth in the United Kingdom may have been especially retarded where its full attainment required the separation of employees. This constraint need not affect industries contracting slowly enough for their labour forces to be reduced by natural attrition. We assume that a reduction of roughly 2 per cent can on average be effected without discharges, which would allow an industry to reduce its workforce by 1977 to 83 per cent of its 1968 level.

For an industry that contracted so fast that employment could not be reduced just through natural wastage, we expect that the output elasticity of labour will be depressed, and the estimated value of β will be reduced.[8] To test this, we constructed a dummy $D = 1$ for any British industry whose employment level was subject to rapid contraction (in the sense just defined), zero otherwise. There were 24 such industries in the United Kingdom, eight of which also contracted employment in the United States by at least 17 per cent. We then added to the basic model (equation (1) of table 6.4) two variables $CAPGD = CAPG*D$ and $TPGD = TPG*D$. (An intercept shift was also tested but eliminated after proving totally insignificant.) In equation (2) of table 6.4 this manoeuvre doubles the explanatory power of the model, and the coefficient of $CAPGD$ is negative as expected. Although not significant, this coefficient implies that the net effect of $CAPG$ is substantially reduced to $0.147 = 0.381 - 0.234$. If $CAPSG$ is added to equation (2) its coefficient is destabilised, suggesting that the UK/US difference is substantially associated with the plight of these declining industries. Notice also the significant negative coefficient of $TPGD$, which makes the net coefficient of TPG go negative: workforce shrinkage is not consistent with attaining economies of scale.

WERE BRITISH INDUSTRIES CATCHING UP?

The principal link between the analysis of comparative productivity growth and productivity levels lies in the question of whether British industries were falling behind or catching up to the productivity levels of their American counterparts during 1968–77, the period between our two cross-sections.

Methods of modelling catch-up

The key lies in the term $EFFG$ in equation (2). Traditionally, the A parameter in the Cobb-Douglas production function is associated with shifts in the function due to disembodied technical progress. In turn, this can be broken down into best-practice progress and diffusion towards (or away from) the best-practice frontier. If we assume the existence of a global best-practice frontier that moves out by the same amount for every country, then $EFFG$ reflects the differential in diffusion rates between the United Kingdom and the United States.[9] This raises the possibility of modelling $EFFG$ as the result of a simple (net) diffusion process.

The most convenient way of doing this is to assume:

$$A_{1K}/A_{1S} = (A_{oK}/A_{oS})^b \qquad (3)$$

Then, if $b = 1$ the 'technology gap' remains constant over time. If $A_{oK}/A_{oS} < 1$, then the gap narrows if $b < 1$ and widens if $b > 1$.[10]

Substituting (3) into $EFFG$, defined as $(A_{1K}/A_{oK})/(A_{1S}/A_{oS})$

$$\log EFFG = (b-1) \log (A_{oK}/A_{oS}) \qquad (4)$$

Thus, $VPWG$ depends on the initial value of EFF, which will attract a positive coefficient if $b > 1$ (that is, British industries are falling further behind), in which case the best performers will be those who were least behind in the first place (that is, enjoyed larger values of A_{oK}/A_{oS}). On the other hand, if diffusion is occurring and bringing up the laggards, $b < 1$

and the best performers will be industries that were most behind in the first place (that is, low A_{oK}/A_{oS}); they have the most to gain from diffusion.

The initial value of *EFF* can be incorporated into the model in three ways. First, it can be measured from the model of relative productivity levels for 1968, estimated in Chapter 3. Specifically, it becomes the residuals from our preferred model (table 3.4) but with only the neoclassical core variables utilised in the residuals calculation. Secondly, the determinants of *EFF* that were specified and tested in preceding chapters (such as labour relations, trade exposure, R&D) can be taken over and entered as explanatory variables in the model determining *VPWG*. Either approach suffers the limitation common to our whole procedure of imposing the same *b* value on all industries. As in the model developed in Chapter 2, we can relax this constraint in a cross-section approach in the *ad hoc* fashion of allowing for differential shifts in particular subsectors of manufacturing. We can also employ a third procedure, described in detail below, of estimating a separate *b* for each industry.

Results

In equation (3) of table 6.4 we employ the first approach, entering *EFF* as the logarithmic residuals from the 1967/8 neoclassical core equation. Its coefficient is negative, indicating that British industries were on balance catching up. Its coefficient does not attain the conventional confidence level for rejecting the null hypothesis, but in various respecifications its t-value always exceeds 1. (The low significance is no surprise given the constraint of imposing the same catch-up rate on all industries.) The other coefficients of equation (3) are very similar to those in the similarly specified equation (2).

Equation (4) modifies the specification by reintroducing the slope shift for *CAPG* in the United States, *CAPSG*, which proved weakly significant in equation (1). Its significance increases somewhat, as does the explanatory power of the model as a whole. Finally, we experimented with a variety of sectoral slope shifts analogous to those entered into our model for productivity levels. As in the model of productivity levels, most evidence of sectoral differences in production functions centres on the chemicals, electrical engineering, and building materials sectors. However, in the model of table 6.4, only the last of these attracted a t-value > 1, and only *BMCAPG* appears in the preferred specification, equation (5).

We can pause to notice the estimates of the production-function parameters implied by equation (5). We now obtain:

	a	β	$a+\beta$
United Kingdom	0.433	0.784	1.227
United States	0.222	1.005	1.227

With catch-up effects controlled, we retain the conclusion that the United Kingdom exhibits lower output-elasticity for labour and higher output-

Table 6.5. *Determinants of relative productivity growth, 61 matched industries, including determinants of level of relative efficiency*

Independent variables	Equation (1)	Equation (2)
Constant	-0.215^a	-0.258^a
	(2.91)	(2.81)
CAPG	0.490^a	0.620^a
	(3.63)	(2.94)
TPG	0.201^a	0.211^a
	(2.70)	(2.77)
CAPSG	0.224	0.320
	(1.41)	(2.60)
TPGD	-0.236^{cc}	-0.244^{cc}
	(1.89)	(1.94)
BMCAPG	-0.584^{cc}	-0.671^{bb}
	(1.91)	(2.05)
UNION	-0.168^b	-0.193^b
	(1.66)	(1.80)
MGRK	0.218^b	0.219^b
	(1.92)	(1.91)
FOSK	0.367^a	0.359^a
	(2.57)	(2.48)
R^2	0.417	n.a.
$\bar{R}^2$	0.328	n.a.

Note: Equation (1) is estimated by ordinary least squares, equation (2) by instrumental variables. Where one-tail tests of significance are appropriate, a = 1 per cent; b = 5 per cent; c = 10 per cent. Where two-tail tests are appropriate, aa = 1 per cent; bb = 5 per cent; cc = 10 per cent.

elasticity for capital than the United States. But the extent of scale economies now appears to be the same in the two countries. For shrinking British industries the substantial negative interaction with scale effects is still apparent.

The second option for modelling the catch-up effect is to replace *EFF* with the variables identified in Chapter 3 as determining it. The candidates include both the variables that actually turned out to wield significant influences in the model of productivity levels in 1967/8 and those nominated for the model on the basis of theory or independent evidence but that failed to prove significant. Equation (1) of table 6.5 presents the result of our experiments with these variables. Of the former group three turned out to have no explanatory power: the United Kingdom industry's exposure to trade (*IMEXK*), residual bellicosity (*BEL*), and research and development (*RD*). However, unionisation (*UNION*) did, as did the management-intensity of the United Kingdom industry (*MGRK*) and foreign subsidiaries' share in the British industry (*FOSK*).

That unionisation levels at the beginning of the period constrained British industries' subsequent rates of relative productivity growth while management intensity supported catch-up, importantly amplifies our findings on these variables in Chapter 3. Independent evidence on the effects of unionisation is certainly consistent with its constraining effect falling heavily on managers' efforts to attain productivity advances. And, while we found indirect evidence that management is ineffective in large-scale British industries, it also appears that the more management-intensive industries in the United Kingdom have shown some capacity for catching up. The evidence that foreign investment serves as a transmission belt for assisting the international diffusion of innovations and productivity improvements within an industry also holds considerable interest and confirms results previously reported for Canada (Globerman, 1979) and Australia (Caves, 1974).

Simultaneous model

Because of the potential significance of these results, we wanted to make sure that they did not reflect incorrect inferences due to simultaneous relations involving productivity growth and the growth of various inputs, outputs, and prices. Therefore, we embedded equation (1) of table 6.5 in a simultaneous system with the following general form:

$$VPWG = f_1 \text{ (as above)}$$
$$CAPG = f_2 \text{ (}OUTG, WAGEG, \text{ labour relations, and so on)}$$
$$TPG = f_3 \text{ (}OUTG, MGR, \text{ labour relations, and so on)}$$
$$OUTG = f_4 \text{ (}PRICEG, IMEXK, FOSK, \text{ sectoral dummies)}$$
$$PRICEG = f_5 \text{ (}VPWG, WAGEG, RD, \text{ labour relations, market structure).}$$

The notation for proportional changes in real output, wages, and relative prices is self-explanatory; MGR refers to relative UK/US management intensity. The resulting equation for $VPWG$ is reported as equation (2) in table 6.5. As can be seen, the estimation of this equation by instrumental variables causes very little change in either the magnitudes of coefficients or their levels of significance, and the conclusions summarised above continue to stand.

While the other equations of the system will not be reported here, a few results hold enough interest to deserve brief mention. Relative capital intensity ($CAPG$) seems to have been higher in industries afflicted by difficult labour relations, as BEL and $UNION$ proved weakly significant with positive coefficients. This result is underlined by the fact that the relative rate of output growth ($OUTG$) did not prove at all significant as a determinant of $CAPG$ or TPG.

Inter-industry differences in growth of efficiency

Our third option for investigating catching-up involves estimating b separately for each industry from the estimates of EFF and $EFFG$,[11] allowing a direct examination of the patterns that they display. We can proceed with this by plotting log *EFFG* against log *EFF* (see chart 6.1). We can compartmentalise this space by noting that if log *EFFG* = − log *EFF*, the British industry's efficiency matches that of the United States at the end of the period.[12] This relation gives rise to the downward sloping 45-degree line in the diagram. Combined with the vertical and horizontal axes, it generates the six possible cases that are summarised in table 6.6.

As the table shows, all but a handful of the 61 industries are in sections III and IV, exhibiting lagging productivity and either closing the gap or falling behind during 1968–77. However, a few interesting cases lie outside these sections. Six industries[13] held leads in efficiency over their American counterparts in 1968, 1977, or both. Efficiency, it should be recalled, has here been normalised for differences in capital intensity and plant scale (in neither year did any British industry approach its American counterpart's unadjusted labour productivity).

Another conclusion from chart 6.1 is that 75 per cent of the sample appear to have fallen further behind their American counterparts during 1968–77. At first sight this seems at odds with our finding (table 6.4,

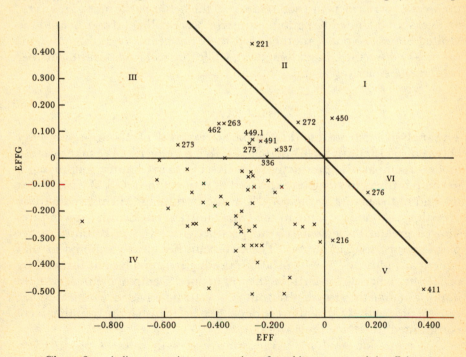

Chart 6.1 *A diagrammatic representation of catching-up: growth in efficiency against initial efficiency*

Source: Estimated residuals from regression analysis.

Table 6.6. *Analysis of relative levels and growth rates of efficiency, 61 matched industries, 1967/8–1977*

Section	EFF	EFFG	Number of industries	Description
I	>0	>0	1	UK increased a lead already established in 1968
II	$\begin{cases} <0 \\ >-EFFG \end{cases}$	>0	2^a	UK lagged in 1968 but overtook US by 1977
III	$<-EFFG$	>0	7^a	UK lagged in 1968 but partly closed gap by 1977
IV	<0	<0	45	UK lagged in 1968 and fell further behind by 1977
V	$\begin{cases} >0 \\ <-EFFG \end{cases}$	<0	2	UK lost a lead held in 1968
VI	$>-EFFG$	<0	1	UK lead in 1968 was retained but reduced in 1977

[a]Three industries fall on the border between II and III.

equation (5)) that the impact of *EFF* on *VPWG* is negative. In fact there is no contradiction: the latter establishes a slight tendency for catching-up by the weaker performers in 1968 relative to the better performers. However, on average all United Kingdom industries were falling further behind the United States. To put it another way, there has been a regression towards the mean within the United Kingdom, while that mean was drifting further behind the American mean.

SUMMARY

The analysis is extended to the comparative growth of labour productivity between 1968 and 1977 in 61 matched UK/US industries. We take over the model of comparative productivity levels set forth in Chapter 2, applying it to comparative growth rates expressed as ratios of the levels of variables at the end of the period to their levels at the beginning. Mean productivity growth was about the same in the two countries, but British growth rates showed greater dispersion (as did productivity levels in Britain's large-plant sectors, see Chapter 5). The two countries clearly differed in that American industries' growth of labour productivity involved little shedding of labour, whereas for Britain the reduction of employment was more important than the growth of output. The statistical evidence indicates that rates of productivity growth were depressed for British industries that were constrained to reduce their workforces.

Our regression analysis of the relative growth rates of productivity strongly supports the productivity-constraining force of labour shedding. Overall, the output elasticity of labour is much lower in the United Kingdom than in the United States when estimated from comparative growth rates, and the output elasticity of capital is much higher. But the difference is further inflated for those sectors subject to significant shedding of labour in the United Kingdom. Moreover, the attainment of scale economies in these sectors seems to have been severely hampered.

Various methods were employed to ascertain whether the worst-performing British industries were seizing the opportunity to catch up to their American counterparts in efficiency (productivity corrected for capital intensity) or, alternatively, were falling further behind. Although the majority of British industries did fall further behind during the period, there was a weak tendency for those lagging the most to catch up with the pack. When we investigated the structural correlates of industries' comparative performance in raising efficiency, we found that the prevalence of union membership retarded productivity performance whereas it increased with the management-intensity of the United Kingdom industry and the prevalence of foreign subsidiaries in the British market.

The first two findings bear an important relation to our earlier conclusions. Troubled labour relations showed some tendency to impair the level of productivity in the late 1960s, and also to retard its growth in the subsequent decade. Many analyses of labour relations preceding ours suggested that British institutional conditions were likely to constrain both the level and the growth rate of productivity, and this parallel evidence on growth and 1967/8 levels inclines us to play down the qualification implied by our finding that labour-relations variables had no effect (or even a perverse effect) on productivity in 1977.

The better productivity-growth performance of industries that are management-intensive in the United Kingdom clearly provides an encouraging counter to the evidence of managerial failure cited in Chapter 1. The hypothesis of managerial failure suggests that productivity gaps may widen over time in industries that are management-intensive – whether in the United Kingdom or elsewhere – and it is reassuring that we can reject this corollary with a high degree of confidence. That multinational companies serve as significant transmission belts for productivity improvement is consistent with this favourable performance in management-intensive British industries.

7

CONCLUSIONS AND POLICY IMPLICATIONS

This study has sought to establish conclusions about productivity in Britain's manufacturing sector by matching individual industries to their counterparts in the United States and explaining differences in the matched industries' levels and rates of growth of labour productivity. The approach provides us with leverage against some hypotheses about the bases for Britain's poor productivity performance that can otherwise be tested indirectly at best. The implications of our findings are explored in this chapter. First, we set forth the quantitative importance that our statistical results impute for each source of the productivity shortfall. Then we draw some procedural lessons for thinking about productivity and ways to improve it that are cast up by our research design. Finally, we adduce the study's implications for various areas of public policy.

QUANTITATIVE IMPLICATIONS OF FINDINGS ON PRODUCTIVITY SHORTFALL

The emphasis of our study so far has fallen upon the testing of hypotheses: determining which factors do, and which do not, make statistically significant contributions to explaining levels and growth rates of productivity. The range of significant factors has turned out to be fairly extensive: capital intensity, plant size, labour relations, education, research outlays, international competitive pressures, and other variables all have roles to play.[1] What we now require is some quantitative assessment of the relative importance of these various influences.

Inter-industry differences in productivity performance

Given the nature of our research design, the question on which we can provide the most direct answer is why some British industries have performed better than others (always, of course, relative to their American counterparts). On this question, we shall not provide a lengthy survey of all our results, but rather opt here for the following presentational device in order to highlight some of our more striking findings. Table 7.1 lists the eight industries in the sample (of 94) that exhibited the highest and lowest values of net output per head relative to their American counterparts. These lists reflect the hypotheses upon which our analysis has focussed:

Table 7.1. *Matched UK/US industries with highest and lowest ratios of UK/US net output per head, 1977*

Highest	Lowest
1 Gramophone records and tapes	1 Toilet preparations
2 Building bricks	2 Cans and metal boxes
3 Mineral oil refining	3 Broadcast receiving/sound reproducing equipment
4 Lubricating oils and greases	4 Linoleum and plastic floor coverings
5 Wooden containers	5 Electric equipment for motor vehicles
6 Agricultural machinery, tractors	6 Telephone, telegraph apparatus
7 Trailers, caravans, freight containers	7 Paper and board
8 Electronic computers	8 Motor vehicles

large-scale assembly industries at the low end, small-scale and/or process industries at the top. When we take geometric averages of relative labour productivity for these groups, the best performers are found to achieve 61 per cent of their American counterparts' productivity, the worst performers only 26 per cent.

Our statistical model sought to explain the differences in productivity performance among these and other sampled manufacturing industries. One indicator of our degree of success is how close the average *explained* differences among these industries come to the actual differences. For the high performers our model predicted average comparative British productivity 49 per cent of their American level; for the worst performers, the model predicted 31 per cent. Thus, although a good deal of the actual gap (between 61 and 26) remains unexplained, the predicted difference (between 49 and 31) indicates something of the model's power to find what distinguishes the leaders from the laggards.

The 49–31 per cent gap flows from the variables in our model that systematically discriminate between the better and worse performers. Accordingly, we expect that the mean values of these discriminating factors will differ considerably between the strong and weak performers listed in table 7.1. Table 7.2 illustrates them by reporting for each factor the ratio of values for the top and bottom performers. The top performers' capital intensity (relative to their American counterparts) was 82 per cent higher than the weakest industries, and their capital intensity in Britain alone was 47 per cent higher. We found that scale economies at the plant level generally contribute to superior productivity; however, with that controlled, the shortcomings specific to large-plant industries in Britain are so strong that the leaders' median plant sizes (employment) are only 25 per cent of the laggards. Strong performers face 42 per cent more international competition in Britain than do the weak ones, and they do 62 per cent more research and development relative to their American counterparts. There

Table 7.2. *Average differences between matched industries with highest and lowest relative net output per head in selected explanatory variables, 1977*

Explanatory variable	Ratio of average for highest to average for lowest industries
Relative capital intensity (*CAP*)	1.827
UK capital intensity (*CAPK*)	1.470
Relative typical plant size (*TP*)	3.407
UK typical plant size (*TPK*)	0.260
Foreign trade exposure (*IMEXK*)	1.416
Relative research intensity (*RD*)	1.624
Relative educational capital[a] (*ED*)	1.005

[a]With the exception of *ED*, these variables are measured as described in Appendix II. The figures shown here refer to the geometric mean value of each variable for the highest productivity industries to that for the lowest productivity industries. For this table only, *ED* is the ratio of UK/US years of schooling.

is little difference, however, in the relative amounts of human capital in their workforces. These factors together make up 87 per cent of the 49–31 gap that we could explain; minor factors account for the balance.

Implications for the overall gap

On a purely academic level, we might draw our survey to a close at this point. We have, after all, gone a long way towards our original objective of identifying the sources of inter-industry differences. However, with the typical American industry producing two and one-half times its British counterpart's net output per head, the inferred sources of the overall gap and what they indicate about the scope for improvement hold great importance for setting policy and anticipating future developments. To evaluate how much we have uncovered of the factors explaining the gap, we must restate the strengths and weaknesses of our research design for that purpose. On the one hand, we obtained in Chapters 3 and 4 estimates of the determinants of productivity that pertain to a broad sample of manufacturing industries and prove robust (with stated exceptions) over the period of a decade. On the other hand, conclusions about inter-industry differences do not automatically translate into conclusions about differences in economy-wide means.

To appreciate this limitation, consider the following stylisation of the problem. Suppose that we can partition the determinants of the productivity gap for any industry into two sets. Set A comprises industry-specific variables: variables that vary in their impact between industries. Amongst other things, this set will include the explanatory variables in our regression equations. Set B, on the other hand, comprises factors that affect the whole economy and do not vary among industries – or do not vary in ways that we could identify with our model. Set B might include a multitude of general national differences between the United Kingdom and the United States that are often suggested as root causes of sluggish British performance, for example, sociological, political and historical factors and possibly macroeconomic dimensions such as the tax system, the nature of demand management, and so on. By definition the variables in Set B are irrelevant to an understanding of the causes of inter-industry variations in labour productivity, because they affect all industries. Their impact is reflected in the magnitude of the overall, or average, gap. Set A variables, on the other hand, are entirely responsible for the explained component of inter-industry variation, but they may or may not contribute to the average as well.[2]

For example, we know that relative capital intensity varies between industries and, from our results, is an important determinant of variations in the productivity gap. However, it is still possible that *on average* capital intensity is broadly similar in the two countries, in which case this variable will be irrelevant for explaining the overall or average gap. However, if in addition to inter-industry variations, the United Kingdom's capital intensity on average falls short of the United States, it should be possible to employ our regressions results to calculate how much of the average productivity gap is due to this factor.

There is more than one way to extract the implications of our findings for the overall productivity shortfall, as the following two questions indicate. First, by how much would the average gap be reduced if each British industry exactly matched its American counterpart with respect to all the explanatory variables in our model? Secondly, by how much would the average gap be reduced if each British industry came as close to its American counterpart as seems feasible, on the basis of the best-performing British industries?

Gains from attaining equality

We develop the former 'equality' approach first. An answer to this question would be simple to compute if all the explanatory variables were specified in terms of UK/US differentials and if the data for the two countries were exactly comparable. Then we could merely calculate the ratio of UK/US net output per head predicted by our equations with all explanatory variables set equal to zero. In fact this would be shown directly as the value of the regression's intercept term. This is the basis for our approach to answering the equality question.

Unfortunately, for the following reasons we can apply this method only partially. First, two of our variables, exposure of the United Kingdom industry to exports and imports, and typical plant size in the United Kingdom industry, are not concerned with comparative effects, and it would be meaningless to insert zero values. Second, our measure of disruptive labour relations is constructed in such a way that its mean value is zero by definition.[3] Therefore, evaluating the equation with the variable set equal to zero does not signify equal disharmony in industrial relations but merely the average experience. (Since we do not know what numerical value of the indicator signifies equal disharmony, this method can tell us nothing about the contribution of disharmony to the average gap.) Third, in collecting data for all our explanatory variables, our main concern was to measure each variable consistently among the industries in each country. We are reasonably confident that this aim was achieved, but less certain that the British and American figures are directly comparable. This is of no consequence for our regression analysis, which depends solely on inter-industry variations.[4] But in the present context, this means that a zero value for a comparative variable need not imply UK/US equality.

We could not investigate the possibility that subtle differences in data-collection methods affect the international comparability of various explanatory variables, but we are aware of serious problems only for the relative stocks of educational and physical capital per worker. For educational capital we suspect that a zero value corresponds to a small excess of the American over the British educational attainment.[5] For physical capital the problem is far more acute, mainly because we have no reliable way to convert figures on United States capital stock into sterling. For this and other reasons[6] it would be reckless to try to estimate the value of relative physical–capital intensity that corresponds to UK/US equality, and so we decided not to include an assessment of the role of capital intensity.

Bearing in mind these points we modify the method by excluding this group of variables from the calculations and replacing them by their sample mean values. The excluded variables are relative physical–capital intensity (and slope shifts for certain sectors), the measure of relative labour disharmony, typical plant size in Britain, and the United Kingdom industry's exposure to international trade.[7] The remaining variables are explored in the manner described above. As a first step, we compute the sample mean of relative net output per head for our dependent variable, and obtain 0.395 for 1967/8 and 0.396 for 1977. These values indicate the magnitude of the average productivity gap: that is, on average the United Kingdom lags by about 60 per cent. Next, we re-express the regression equation with selected variables evaluated at their sample means. The resulting equations for 1967/8 and 1977 are shown in table 7.3. The revised intercept terms[8] show the predicted values of relative net output per head corresponding to UK/US equality for the explanatory variables appearing in table 7.3. The adjusted values are 0.583 for 1967/8 and 0.539 for 1977.[9] In other words if, somehow, British industry were able to match the United

Table 7.3. *'Best' ordinary least squares model of determinants of relative labour productivity, re-estimated for analysis of closing the productivity gap*

Explanatory variable	Estimated coefficients 1967/8	1977
Intercept term	−0.550	−0.638
Differential female workforce percentage (*PCF*)	−0.362	−0.176
Differential part-time percentage (*PART*)	−1.148	−0.826
Differential non-production operatives (*NOPS*)	−0.394	—
Differential human capital per head (*ED*)	+0.156	+0.099
Differential union membership (*UNION*)	−0.133	—
Relative research expenditure (*RD*)	+0.024	—
Relative typical plant size (*TP*)	—	+0.092
Relative typical plant size, electrical and instrument engineering (*ELTP*)	+0.371	+0.047

Note: These results are derived from the equations reported in table 3.4 with the intercept terms re-estimated setting the following variables at their sample mean values: *TPK*, *BEL*, *IMEXK*, *CAP*, *CHECAP*, *ELCAP*, and *BMCAP*, and *CAPK* (for 1977 only).

States with respect to these factors (with capital intensity, absolute plant size, degree of overseas competition, and industrial disharmony remaining unchanged at current levels), on average its productivity would increase to between 53 and 58 per cent of the comparable American level.

In table 7.4 we report the percentage changes in relative net output per head predicted to result from a move to equality for each variable separately (holding all others at their current sample means). As can be seen, for 1967/8 all of the variables except union membership contribute positively to the overall improvement, but the major sources result from relative human capital, relative part-time employment[10] and scale economies in the electrical and instrument engineering sector. The result concerning the last variable requires elaboration in two respects. First, the figure shown is net of a small reverse effect associated with the increase in typical United Kingdom plant size (which has a negative effect on relative net output per head implied by increasing relative plant scale in this sector).[11] Secondly, this variable applies to only a small proportion of the sample industries, and so the contribution of this factor to the aggregate 58 per cent improvement for 1967/8 is much more modest than 19 per cent.[12] Nevertheless, this result does suggest the potential for major gains from increased plant size within the electrical and instrument engineering industries.

For 1977, differential female workforce participation, part-time work, educational capital, and research outlays each has a lesser effect, but their relative importance is unchanged, with part-time working and (especially) human capital dominating.[13] On the other hand, relative typical plant size enters explicitly in 1977 unlike in 1968. The figure shown reflects the *net*

Table 7.4. *Predicted percentage improvements in relative net output per head resulting from movement of exogenous variables, 1967/8 and 1977*

Exogenous variable	1967/8		1977	
	Equality	Best practice	Equality	Best practice
Differential female workforce percentage (*PCF*)	2.5	3.6	1.0	1.6
Differential part-time percentage (*PART*)	8.8	8.4	8.2	5.1
Differential non-production percentage (*NOPS*)	1.2	3.2	0.0	0.0
Differential human capital per head (*ED*)	22.2	8.5	13.7	5.9
Differential research expenditure (*RD*)	1.5	4.7	0.2	4.1
Differential union membership (*UNION*)	−1.0	3.6	0.0	0.0
Relative labour antagonism (*BEL*)	n.a.	3.1	n.a.	3.9
Trade exposure, UK industry (*IMEXK*)	n.a.	5.4	n.a.	6.0
Typical plant size, UK industry (*TPK*)	n.a.	5.5[a]	n.a.	1.0
Relative typical plant size[b] (*TP*)	0 (or 19.0)	0 (or 19.6)	−0.2 (or 4.6)	(or 5.6)[c]
Relative physical capital per head[d] (*CAP*)	n.a.	9.1	n.a.	9.2

[a]This figure is net in that it corresponds to a reduction in UK plant sizes resulting in a 12 per cent increase in *VPW* via *TPK*, 11 per cent of which is offset by the negative effect this has via a reduction in *TP*.
[b]For all industries excluding those in *EL*.
[c]The figures in parentheses apply only to industries in *EL*.
[d]This is a weighted average of the following: for 1967/8: 32.8 per cent for industries in chemicals (*CHE*), 0.0 per cent (*EL*), 0.7 per cent (*BM*), 8.6 per cent (all other industries); for 1977: 20.7 per cent (*CHE*), 3.65 per cent (*EL*), 2.4 per cent (*BM*), 8.6 per cent (all other industries). Also, for 1977 the figure reflects the joint effort of *CAP* and *CAPK*.

effect of increasing British plant sizes to their American counterpart levels: it is negative because the positive effect of increasing *relative* plant size is just outweighed by the corresponding negative effect of an increase in *absolute* typical plant size in Britain. As in 1968, the net effect is positive in the electrical and instrument engineering sector, but is much reduced.

Gains from attaining best practice

We now turn to an alternative approach to expressing the implications of our estimated coefficients for the sources of productivity shortfall. The preceding set of estimates is tempered by no constraint on the feasibility of bringing the factors determining British industries' productivity up to the levels of their American counterparts. However, our statistical model does offer a rough but reasonable indication of what relative performance is feasible for the typical British industry in the dispersion of relative values for the exogenous variables in the sample. That is, we focus on a level of performance which is materially superior to the average but which, nevertheless, has been attained by some British industries in the sample. For convenience of expression we shall refer to this level as the *best practice* (which may or may not imply a level greater than the American average). We measure this best-practice level for each variable by the sample mean ± one standard deviation: + for variables with positive coefficients, − otherwise. We then proceed exactly as in the first method, but this time investigating the consequences of moving from the sample mean to best practice rather than to equality with the United States.

The use of one standard deviation is admittedly arbitrary. However, one can be fairly confident that the change involved is feasible inasmuch as it involves a level that has already been attained by some United Kingdom industries. Also, it is sufficiently moderate to carry only a small risk of identifying best practice with outlying observations that might result from freak conditions or measurement error.[14]

Substituting the best-practice values for all explanatory variables into our best model for 1967/8, we secure a predicted value for relative net output per head of 0.682.[15] Compared to the observed actual sample mean (0.395), this implies a 72.6 per cent increase in British productivity. For 1977 the predicted value is 0.575, which implies an increase of 45.6 per cent. Thus, the scope for improvement lying within the range of best practice as we have defined it seems quite substantial.[16]

In order to assess the contribution made to this figure by each explanatory variable, as for the first method, we have recalculated the improvement corresponding to a change in each variable separately (in each case all others being held at their sample mean values). The results are shown in the columns of table 7.4 headed 'best practice'. Comparing the figures for the variables which we could also investigate using the first method, the most obvious difference that we find for 1967/8 is the more restrained influence of relative human capital intensity (which reflects the fact that equality with the United States would involve a level of educational input in excess of anything actually observed in the sample). On the other hand, differential research spending, non-production operatives, female employment percentage, and union membership each contribute more substantially in this method of assessment (the turnaround of union membership is associated with a reduction of unionisation). Interestingly, the combined influence of these seven variables is to increase relative net output per head by 38.8 per cent, which is not greatly out of line with their contribution for 1967/8 using the equality method. Among the four variables that we could not examine by the equality method, the most important is capital intensity, which is subject to considerable variation among sectors, although absolute plant size, overseas competition, and disharmony all contribute significantly. For 1977 the differences between the contributions estimated by the two methods are very similar to those for 1967/8.

In summary, if one is prepared to attach some credibility to hypothetical calculations of this nature, two broad conclusions emerge. First, the fear, expressed earlier, that our econometric approach merely identifies peripheral factors but not the crux of the problem of low productivity in British manufacturing, seems to be unfounded. While our calculations implicitly suggest a very important additional role for what we called Set B factors (which are outside the scope of our methodology), they also suggest that much of the overall productivity gap is sensitive to the variables that we have identified. Secondly, within this set of factors, there is no outstanding single variable at which the finger can be pointed: although some are clearly more important than others, the picture to emerge is of a steady cumulation of influences of, in some cases, quite different origins responsible for low British productivity.

LESSONS FOR ANALYSING PRODUCTIVITY

Our model and quantitative results contain many lessons for the analysis of productivity and methods of improving it. While some may be obvious to one who has thought carefully about the analytical foundations of efficient use of resources, they are violated with great regularity in public discussions. Raising productivity is a goal that carries the sanctified status of a good thing, yet many a proposed measure to raise productivity may well fail to represent an efficient use of resources.

First of all, productivity is often measured in the fashion of our model as output per unit of labour input. Yet almost any production process requires the combining of labour services with substantial quantities of other inputs, including capitalised investments in education and training to improve the quality of labour's services. The concept of productivity on which we should ideally focus for policy purposes is total factor productivity, a ratio of value of output to a weighted index of the costs of all inputs. Total factor productivity is not readily calculated,[17] of course, and that is why the neoclassical core of our model was developed in order to bridge the gap between labour productivity and total factor productivity.

Formal models of productivity (Farrell, 1957) customarily distinguish between the technical efficiency of a production process ('Could we secure the same output with less of all inputs?') and allocative or price efficiency ('Could we produce the same output at lower cost with a different combination of inputs?'). Our model and statistical results embody this same distinction, which appeared above as a distinction between the influences contained in the neoclassical core model and those that test hypotheses about efficiency. Strictly speaking, the neoclassical core model does not yield any direct conclusions about whether a given sector, or even United Kingdom manufacturing as a whole, employs an inefficient combination of inputs. As we remarked in Chapter 1, while increasing the capital intensity of British manufacturing would raise labour productivity, it would not necessarily increase output by more than the opportunity cost of the capital: capital intensity tends to be low because British labour is cheap, and the net revenue gains from replacing it with capital services are correspondingly attenuated.

It should also be kept in mind that our industry-level figures reflect average productivity, whereas the allocation of resources is optimised at the margin. Resources allocated to research and development, for example, may on average earn excess returns that are due to intra-marginal rents and hence do not necessarily indicate the presence of opportunities at the margin for profitably diverting resources to this use.

What can we conclude about a factor in the neoclassical core that takes a large and statistically significant coefficient – large in the sense of gains from attaining best-practice? Such a result issues a broad-based warning that matched British and American industries differ substantially in how they combine resources, raising the probability that *at least one* of the two countries suffers from substantial deficiencies in the production, pricing, or allocation of the input in question. The exact nature of the deficiency and the best way to repair it then require further inquiry into the prices, marginal products, and opportunity costs of the factor in question. The detailed inquiries of Prais and others into vocational education and the production of labour skills in Britain (and Germany) represent an example of the complementary 'next step' that is indicated.[18]

Our findings about the factors that determine the efficiency of British manufacturing, outside the neoclassical core of the model, require a somewhat different interpretation. Take our central conclusion that managerial and labour-relations factors in conjunction depress British productivity in industries where production is efficiently organised in large plants. A number of conclusions might follow from this finding, although none can be assumed without further evidence. One is behavioural: unless this situation is remedied, market forces in the international economy will induce resources to shift away from such sectors.[19] The conclusions of Chapter 6 coupled with a good deal of indirect evidence from other sources suggest that industries subject to the most important productivity depressants have indeed been subjected to contraction and loss of comparative advantage. A second is that investments in managerial skills (although not, on our evidence, simply adding more managers to the existing bundle of inputs), or in the arbitrage of managerial practice from other countries, might yield a high rate of return. A third is that changes in the contractual framework of labour relations (from what prevailed in 1967/8 and 1977) might be made to yield higher real incomes to all factors of production.

Once again, the implication stands out that measures to improve productivity are never a 'free lunch'. Rather, they are opportunities to use resources in ways that at the margin exceed their opportunity cost.

IMPLICATIONS FOR POLICY

The comments of the previous two sections stand as general background to the policy implications of the study. Without repeating all the cautions and qualifications that they (and our statistical findings as well) require, we shall indicate what our findings generally imply for several major areas of economic policy.

Competition and business organisation

At the plant level, big is not beautiful in Britain, and many efforts to increase the scales of the larger production units would be ill-advised. The same goes for efforts to prevent the decline of mass-production sectors facing international competition, unless some specific opportunities can be identified for overcoming their productivity deficiencies. At the level of enterprise organisation the message of our findings is not so clear. Certainly there is no evidence that producer concentration has a favourable effect on productivity, and in part our findings indicate an unfavourable effect. Given market and plant sizes, higher concentration must on average be associated with larger sizes of enterprises. Our study provides no evidence for (and some evidence against) the prospect of gains from larger scales of business organisation. To that extent it supports policies hostile to industrial concentration.

With regard to international trade, our findings accord with the conventional liberal preference for eschewing restrictions on trade. Indeed, specific evidence that protection fosters or preserves technically inefficient production in the industrial countries has been coming to the fore, first in developing but now in industrialised countries.[20] The urge to employ protection as an employment-creating device should be resisted, and the European Community can claim some virtue as a form of commitment that deters the temptation that this policy holds for national policy (a virtue that, however, may not nearly offset the costs to the United Kingdom of the Common Agricultural Policy).

Human capital

Our results strongly support the charge that the United Kingdom under-invests in human capital. Taking the statistical results in conjunction with evidence reviewed in Chapter 1, we conclude that productivity has suffered from pervasive under-investment in everything from simple technical skills to business administration. The weak technical and administrative training of business managers has been widely criticised. That is borne out in our evidence insofar as the shortfall lies in managerial skills relevant to the plant floor. Our results also show strongly the imprint of low levels of technical skills in the general workforce: a problem less attended in public discussion. While our findings (for reasons noted previously) do not prove that the marginal benefits of additional outlays on worker training would exceed the costs, the indirect implication is strong indeed. The substantial effect of differential human capital found in our results, the seriously limited labour mobility, Britain's slippage in comparative advantage for 'quality' products (reported in other studies) imply either that the nation under-invests in training or that its populace is uneducable.

Labour relations

Our findings for the much-debated issue of British labour relations are in fact rather unclear. For 1967/8 our data seem to indicate that the proportion of employees who are trade-union members on balance had a negative effect on productivity; with that controlled, productivity also suffered from antagonistic labour relations. Our evidence also indicated that the extent of trade-union membership was negatively associated with productivity growth in the 1968–77 decade. Considering our strong finding for both 1967/8 and 1977 of depressed productivity in large plants, where independent evidence indicates that labour organisation and restrictive work rules are widely prevalent, we accept the verdict that trade unions' prevalence is negatively associated with productivity despite the lack of directly confirming evidence in our 1977 cross-section.

Devising remedial policies that are both efficient and socially acceptable is a task that we do not propose to undertake here. We venture only the thought that the effect on productivity of changes in institutions and policies in the early 1980s will be, in the light of our results, most interesting to observe.

Policies toward adjustment and reallocation

A major conclusion flowing from Chapter 6 is that productivity growth in British manufacturing has been attenuated in industries where its faster growth would have involved the shedding of labour. No doubt this pattern reflects the strong reluctance, evident in Britain and Europe as a whole, of labour to change jobs when it involves forsaking a long-familiar workplace and neighbourhood. Economic analysis has generally been reluctant to deal formally with this issue, but it has been recognised recently (Houseman, 1985) that the loss of a job in such circumstances imposes not just the recognised costs of retraining and/or relocation but also a loss due to the increased cost of obtaining those satisfactions formerly supplied by the familiar environment of workplace and neighbourhood. Furthermore, the many public policies observed in the industrial countries that provide workers with limited property rights in their jobs can be rationalised (or at least explained as political choices) as recognising these non-market costs of relocation.

Of course, acknowledging the reality of these non-market costs of relocation does not establish the optimality of any arbitrary policy to forestall the loss of jobs. But it does indicate that the optimal policy is not necessarily one that recognises only the objective costs of reallocation, and it warns us that resistance to job changes may stem from large but unobservable quasi-rents that make workers willing to take part vigorously in rent-preserving activities. Furthermore, it may explain the check on productivity growth that we found associated with labour-shedding in British manufacturing industries.

Besides non-market costs of reallocating labour, many other features of the adjustment process provide potential for useful policy-making. We only note them here because our own research does not address these. The individual private decision-maker's expectations may err systematically about the returns to shifting resources from one sector to another if he fails to anticipate the simultaneous moves of other decision-makers and their combined effect on the sectors' output prices, which a well informed public authority might catch. Or public policy may inadvertantly distort incentives to reallocate resources, as when corporate income-tax provisions cushion the losses run by firms that postpone decisions to reallocate.

One aspect of adjustment policy closely related to Britain's problems is training and retraining in job skills. The evidence indicates that Britain differs from other countries in its investment in labour skills, not only by making low levels of investment but also by making them as specific skills through on-the-job learning. As a result, much of the human capital of the average working person is tied up on specific skills learnt on the job. As an alternative, general education could be continued to a later age and provided with more vocational content, or initial vocational training could be more broadly based. Either option holds out the advantage of greater adaptability for the individual in the face of technological changes. And it offers the potential dividend of reducing resistance to change and softening the defense of restrictive rules by those whose well-being turns on quasi-rents obtained from unduly narrow bases of skill and competence.

The period of investigation for our study ended a decade ago: a reflection of the infrequent collection and long publication lags for some of our most strategic sources of data. In that time many changes highly relevant to our findings have occurred in both the performance of the British manufacturing sector and the policies applied to it. Productivity in manufacturing has grown more rapidly, rising to a pace of 5.1 per cent per annum during

1980–5 from 2.4 per cent during the 1970s. On the other hand, total manufacturing output is 5 per cent lower than in 1979. The incidence of strikes has declined substantially (to about a third of the totals typical in the late 1970s), perhaps in association with the persistence of high unemployment and bankruptcies.

The changes in policies in education are perhaps the most significant in the long run. There has been an increasing recognition of the role of vocational education. But important initiatives such as the expansion of vocational education at schools are still only in a pilot phase and the Youth Training Scheme for school leavers remains in need of substantial strengthening. There is also a longer-term worry that, although there was a substantial increase in the number of university graduates in the 1970s, the resources available for the universities and polytechnics have been significantly reduced since 1981.

In short, while progress in British manufacturing productivity in the past five years gives some grounds for optimism, the productivity gap in relation to other countries remains substantial. The central problem of the present study – how to close the gap – is thus likely to warrant the attention of economic analysts for some time to come.

THE SAMPLE INDUSTRIES

The matched manufacturing industries used in this study were selected on the basis of the information contained in the standard industrial classification manual of Britain and the United States, employed for the United Kingdom *Report on the Census of Production*, 1968 and 1977, and the United States 1967 *Census of Manufactures*, 1967 and 1977.

Starting from the United Kingdom's minimum list headings (MLH), all manufacturing industries were included in the sample that could be matched closely and that did not represent 'miscellaneous' or 'not elsewhere specified' product groups.

We matched 87 industries in this way for 1967/8. In 1977 we were able to increase this number to 101 for two reasons: first, the American 1977 Census classification embodied some relatively minor revisions which worked to our advantage, and secondly the British 1977 Census included disaggregations of some 3-digit into 4-digit industries (for example, MLH 333 was split into 333.1, 333.2 and 333.3). Not only did this provide us with *more* matched industries, but also improved and finer comparability in these cases.

In the event, for twelve of our industries in 1967/8 and seven in 1977, appropriate data on key explanatory variables were unattainable and these industries, bracketed in table A.1, are excluded from all experiments reported in the text. This leaves an effective sample of 74 industries in 1967/8, rising to 94 in 1977.

Data availability provided a somewhat larger problem when investigating productivity growth, 1968–77. Starting from the set of industries which could be matched in both 1968 and 1977, and whose definitions were unchanged through the period, we included in our sample only those for which indices of output and input growth were available in both countries. Thus the data used were not merely first differences of the 1968 and 1977 data sets. (As explained in the first section of Chapter 6, we feared that such a procedure would not satisfactorily disentangle real from nominal changes.) In fact, the numbers of industries with available independent indices of real outputs and inputs was only 61, and these are indicated in the last column of the table.

Table A.1. *The sample industries: a concordance between the United Kingdom and the United States standard industrial classifications*

Industry name	MLH no.	US SIC (67)	US SIC (77)	1968	1977	1968–77
1 Grain milling	211		2041,3,4	(+)	+	(+)
2 Bread and flour confectionery	212	2051		+	+	+
3 Biscuits	213	2052		+	+	+
4 Bacon curing, meats and fish	214	2013,5; 2031,6	2013,6,7; 2091,2	+	+	(+)
5 Milk and milk products	215	2021–4, 2026		+	+	+
6 Sugar	216	2061–3		(+)		+
7 Cocoa, chocolate, sugar confectionery	217	2071–3	2065–7	+	+	+
8 Fruit and vegetable products	218	2032–5, 2037–8		+	+	+
9 Animal and poultry foods	219	2042	2047,8	+	+	+
10 Vegetable/animal oils and fats	221	2091–4	2074–7	+	+	+
11 Margarine	229.1		2079		+	
12 Starch and miscellaneous foods	229.2		2046; 2095,8,9		+	
13 Brewing and malting	231	2082,3		+	+	
14 Soft drinks	232	2086,7		+	+	+
15 Spirit distilling and compounding	239.1		2085		(+)	
16 Tobacco	240	2111,2121,2131		(+)	(+)	+
17 Mineral oil refining	262	2911, 2999		+	+	+
18 Lubricating oils and greases	263	2992		+	+	+
19 Pharmaceuticals	272	2831,3,4		+	+	+
20 Toilet preparations	273	2844		+	+	+
21 Paint	274	2851		+	+	(+)
22 Soaps and detergents	275	2841		+	+	+
23 Plastic materials and resins	276	2821,2		(+)	+	+
24 Fertilizers	278	2871,2	2873,4	(+)	+	+
25 Polishes	279.1	2842	2842,2879	(+)	+	(+)
26 Adhesives	279.2	2891		(+)	+	+
27 Printing inks	279.5	2893		+	+	
28 Iron and steel	311,312, 261	3112,6,7; 3323; 3567		+		
29 Iron castings	313	3321,2		+		
30 Aluminium	321	3334, 3352, 3361, 3497	3334, 3353 3354, 3361 3497	+	+	
31 Copper, brass	322	3331,3351,3362		+	+	
32 Agricultural machinery, tractors	331,380	3522	3523,4	+	+	
33 Metalworking machine tools	332	3541,2,4,5	3541,2,4,9	+	+	+
34 Pumps	333.1		3561		+	
35 Valves	333.2	3561	3494	+	(+)	
36 Compressors	333.3		3563		+	
37 Industrial engines	334	3511, 3519		+	(+)	(+)

Table A.1. (*cont.*)

Industry name	MLH no.	US SIC (67)	US SIC (77)	1968	1977	1968–77
38 Textile machinery and accessories	335	3552		+	+	+
39 Construction machinery	336	3531		+	+	+
40 Mechanical handling equipment	337	3534–7	3534–6	+	+	+
41 Office machinery	338	3572,4,9		+	+	
42 Mining machinery	339.1	3532		+	+	(+)
43 Printing, paper machinery	339.2	3554–5		+	+	
44 Refrigerating machinery	339.3	3585		(+)	+	+
45 Scales; portable power tools	339.5		3546,3576		+	
46 Food and drink processing machinery	339.7	3551		+	+	
47 Ball and roller bearings	349.1		3562		+	
48 Photographic/document copying equipment	351	3861		+	(+)	+
49 Watches and clocks	352	3871–2	3873	+	+	+
50 Surgical instruments, appliances	353	3841–3,3851		+	+	+
51 Scientific and industrial instruments	354		3832, 3811 3822–5,9		+	
52 Telephone and telegraph apparatus	363	3661		(+)	+	(+)
53 Radio and electronic components	364	3671–4,9	367	+	+	+
54 Gramophone recordings, tapes	365.1		3652		+	
55 Broadcast receiving/ sound reproducing equipment	365.2	3651,2	3651	+	+	+
56 Electronic computers	366	3573		+	+	
57 Radio, radar and electronic capital goods	367	3662	3662,3693	+	+	+
58 Domestic electrical appliances	368	363		+	+	+
59 Electric equipment for motor vehicles	369.1		3647,3694		+	
60 Batteries	369.2		3691,2		+	
61 Shipbuilding, marine engineering	370	3731,2		+		
62 Motor vehicle manufacturing	381.1	3711,3,4,5	3465,3711,3,4	+	+	
63 Trailers, caravans, freight containers	381.2	3791,9; 3461	3715–6; 3792		+	
64 Motor cycles	382	3751		(+)	+	+
65 Engineers' small tools	390		3545		+	
66 Hand tools and implements	391	3423,5		+	+	+
67 Bolts, nuts, screws, rivets	393	3451,2		+	+	+
68 Cans and metal boxes	395	3411		+	+	

Table A.1. (*cont.*)

Industry name	MLH no.	US SIC (67)	US SIC (77)	1968	1977	1968–77
69 Jewellery and precious metals	396		3911,4,5		(+)	
70 Metal furniture	399.1	2514, 2522		+	+	+
71 Man-made fibres	411	2823,4		(+)	+	+
72 Spinning and doubling	412	2281,2,4		+	+	(+)
73 Weaving	413	2211, 2221		+	+	+
74 Woollen and worsted	414		2231,2283,2291		+	
75 Rope, twine and net	416	2298		+	+	+
76 Hosiery and other knitted goods	417.1	2251–4,2256	2251–4,7,9	+	+	+
77 Warp knitting	417.2	2259	2258		+	
78 Lace	418	2292		+	+	+
79 Carpets	419	2271,2,9		+	+	+
80 Narrow fabrics	421	2241		+	+	+
81 Canvas goods	422.2	2393,4		+	+	+
82 Textile finishing	423		2261,2,9		(+)	
83 Leather	431	3111		+	+	+
84 Leather goods	432	3161,3171–2,3199		+	+	+
85 Weatherproof outerwear	441	2385		+	+	(+)
86 Mens' and boys' tailored outerwear	442	2311,2327		+	+	+
87 Overalls and mens' shirts	444	2321–2,2328	2321,2,8,9	+	+	(+)
88 Hats, caps and millinery	446	2351–2		+	+	+
89 Gloves	449.2	2381,3151		+	+	+
90 Footwear	450	3021,3131,3141–2		(+)		+
91 Refractory goods	461.1	3521,5,9	3255,3297	+	+	+
92 Building bricks	461.2		3251,3259		+	
93 Pottery	462	326	3253,326	+	+	+
94 Glass	463	3211; 3221,9;		+	+	+
95 Cement	464	3241		+	+	+
96 Abrasives	469.1	3291		+	+	+
97 Wood containers/baskets	475	244		+	+	+
98 Paper and board	481	2611, 2621 2631, 2641		+	+	+
99 Cardboard boxes	482.1	2651–5		+	+	+
100 Packaging products	482.2	2643		+	+	+
101 Rubber	491	3011, 3069	3011, 3041 3069	(+)	+	+
102 Linoleum, plastic floor coverings	492	3996		+	+	+
103 Brushes and brooms	493	3992	3991	+	+	+
104 Toys, games	494.1	394	3942,4	+	+	+
105 Sports equipment	494.3		3949		+	
106 Stationers' goods	495	395		+	+	+

Sources: United Kingdom, Business Statistics Office, *Report on the Census of Production 1968 and 1977* (HMSO). United States, Bureau of the Census, *1977 Industry and Product Classification Manual* and Executive Office of the President, *Standard Industrial Classification Manual*, Government Printing Office, Washington 1977 and 1972 respectively.

Notes: Unless shown otherwise, the United States classification remained unchanged between 1967 and 1977. Many of the changes which did occur, and are shown, merely involved renumbering of industries, with content unchanged.

+ signs in the last three columns indicate which industries could be matched in principle in each of the data sets. (+) indicates an industry for which data on key explanatory variables were deficient; these industries were therefore excluded from the econometric tests.

Table A.2 provides a check on the representativeness of our samples. It is based on only those industries actually included in the 1977 and 1967/8 regression analyses of chapters 3–5 (that is, 94 and 74 respectively, and excluding those bracketed in the table). The figures shown use net output as the measure of size, although an almost identical picture emerges in aggregate, and across sectors, if employment is used in its place.

In both years and in both countries, the overall coverage comfortably exceeds 50 per cent which is satisfactory for our purposes. It is surprising, at first sight, that coverage is not noticeably higher in 1977 than 1968, bearing in mind the large number of industries included in 1977. This is explained by the fact that many of the extra industries in 1977 resulted from disaggregations of 1968 industries.

Coverage also seems adequate or better within each of the broadly defined sectors shown. The poorest coverage is achieved, fortunately, in the quantitatively less important sectors: Metal goods; Paper etc.; Other Manufacturing (for 1968); and Building Materials etc. (for the United States) and Metal production (for 1977). The order in which the sectors are listed in the table is based on absolute productivity levels in the United Kingdom and, as can be seen, there is no pronounced tendency for the sample to be more or less heavily represented in high or low productivity sectors.

Rather surprisingly the coverage for individual sectors sometimes differs noticeably between the two countries, for example, in 1977 the sample industries account for 60 per cent of the British vehicles sector as opposed to 6 per cent in the American. Since the industries are, of course, identical, this reflects differences in their relative importance in the two countries. Another even more noticeable

Table A.2. *Coverage of the sample*
Net output of the sample industries as a percentage of the population

		1977		1968	
		UK	US	UK	US
Oil and chemicals	(12.4)	59.0	63.0	39.7	50.4
Food, drink, tobacco	(12.9)	80.4	80.7	72.2	72.5
Metals	(5.7)	23.3	20.3	93.9	91.9
Vehicles	(11.9)	60.4	66.2	69.7	54.8
Paper and printing	(8.0)	25.7	32.4	26.6	33.7
Mechanical eng.	(12.7)	50.4	52.5	51.1	52.8
Instrument and electrical eng.	(10.5)	64.9	81.7	58.4	73.4
Metal goods	(6.2)	23.3	20.3	18.5	28.1
Building materials, timber and furniture	(7.3)	39.3	24.6	40.4	29.4
Other manufacturing	(4.4)	58.5	40.7	23.5	19.2
Textiles and clothing	(8.0)	63.7	64.0	46.4	47.4
All manufacturing		53.9	53.9	52.5	53.8

Notes: Figures in brackets after sector name denote shares of all manufacturing in United Kingdom for 1977. Sectors are listed in descending order of productivity in the United Kingdom. The ranking is almost identical using American productivity figures.

example is Oils and Chemicals in 1967/8: because of incompatible industry definitions, our sample excludes all 'General Chemicals' activities. While these activities were *absolutely* important in both countries, they accounted for a smaller proportion of the American sector total because of the greater importance of other industries (for example, Pharmaceuticals and Oil Refining). Notice how this UK/ US differential had narrowed considerably by 1977, presumably due to the increased relative importance of Oil Refining in the United Kingdom.

Given that the structure of sectors does vary between the countries, this differential in coverage is almost inevitable unless the sample approaches 100 per cent. In any event, it does not cause us undue concern, since the sample coverage is at least respectable in all sectors. On the other hand it provides an example of how coverage by industry numbers (identical by definition in the United Kingdom and the United States) can differ from coverage by output share. Digressing just briefly this raises a related issue in the econometric investigations: should observations be unweighted (that is, all industries treated equally), or should they be weighted by industry size? At an early stage in our work, we experimented with both weighted and unweighted least squares regressions on the 1967/8 data set. As there were no substantive differences in the results, we did not pursue weighted regression further.

Finally, we can compare the average productivity in the samples and population. In 1977 in both countries the sample industries were marginally (1 per cent) more productive than the average for the population. Or to put it another way, overall coverage using the employment size measure is slightly lower than that shown for net output. In 1967/8 exactly the same is true for the United States but surprisingly for the United Kingdom the sample industries are slightly less productive (-3 per cent) than the population. This last result is hardly desirable but the difference is sufficiently small to be tolerable. Undoubtedly, it is a manifestation of the differences in within-sector coverage just noted. For example, the overall coverage differences between the output and employment measures in the United Kingdom virtually disappear if we exclude the Oil and Chemicals sector.

Bearing in mind that our sample selection was not random but designed to maximise coverage, we are well pleased with the results shown in the table and are confident that our sample is sufficiently representative to generalise the findings in the main text to the populations from which they arise.

VARIABLE DEFINITIONS AND DATA SOURCES

This appendix provides more details on the specification and measurement of the variables used in the econometric analysis. A more abbreviated checklist is shown at the end of the contents to this volume, and variables are also always defined on the first appearance in the main text.

Our general practice is to specify variables in comparative UK/US form, either as a ratio or as a difference (*denotes the latter below). In some cases however our theoretical framework dictates they be specified as British or American levels. Where this happens in the text we add a K or S to the end of the variable name. In Chapter 6 we employ a rate of change framework and where variables refer to the change between 1968 and 1977 this is denoted by G at the end of the variable name.

Data sources are shown in numeric form after each definition, with a key provided at the end. Occasionally observations on explanatory variables are not available for the year of study and we use an alternative year instead – again this is shown where appropriate below.

Productivity variables

VPW	Value-added (net output) per employee (average number of employees over the year), corrected for price differences. See *PRICE* and note 3 to Chapter 3.
*VPW*1	Value-added per worker in plants of greater than midpoint size (*TP*).
*VPW*2	Value-added per worker in plants of less than midpoint size.
Sources:	A1.2, A3.1; D1.1, D3.1; A1.1, A3.4; D1.2, D3.2.
VPWG	Growth in labour productivity defined as the ratio of an index number for real net output divided by an index number of the labour input in 1977 (base year 1968 for United Kingdom, 1967 for United States).
Sources:	G5, E1.

Capital intensity

CAP	Gross fixed capital stock per employee.
CHECAP, ELCAP and BMCAP	are the same for industries in, respectively; the Chemicals and Oils Sector (nos. 17–27 in table A.1); Electrical and Instrument Engineering (nos. 48–60); Building Materials (nos. 91–96). So, for example, $CHECAP = CAP \times D$ where $D = 1$ for industries 17–27, and $D = 0$ otherwise.
CAPG	Growth in capital intensity defined as the ratio of $CAP77/CAP68$.

CAPGD	is *CAPG* for industries in which United Kingdom employment was subject to rapid contraction 1968–77.
Sources:	A1.2, A3.1; G2, G3; D3.1.

Plant size

TP	Typical plant size as represented by the midpoint (or median of the first moment distribution) plant size (50 per cent of industry employment being accounted for by plants of less than midpoint size). This is derived from Census plant size distribution tables showing the number of plants and employment within certain size classes (the empirical counterpart of the first moment distribution). Estimates are usually based on interpolation within the midpoint size class, or extrapolation on logarithmic probability paper where the midpoint lies in the largest (unbounded) size class. In the few cases where the latter method was necessary, estimates were checked using the alternative assumption of Paret distribution in the largest size class; in a handful of industries these alternative estimates differed importantly and a compromise was used.
ELTP	is *TP* for industries in the Electrical and Engineering Sectors, that is, $ELTP = TP \times D$ when $D = 1$ for industries 48–60, and $D = 0$ otherwise.
TPG	Growth in typical plant size, defined as the ratio of plant size in 1977 to that in 1968. For reasons explained in the second section of Chapter 6 and note 6 to Chapter 6, plant size is measured in this case by the mean size of plants with more than 50 employees.
TPGD	is *TPG* for those industries in which United Kingdom employment was subject to rapid contraction 1968–77.
Sources:	A1.1, A3.4; D1.2, D3.2.

Industry size and growth

SIZE	Industry size measured by sales (*PRICE* corrected). (In ordinary least squares regressions, for econometric reasons, measured by the average of the UK/US ratios of net output and employment, see note 2 to Chapter 4.)
Sources:	A1.2, A3.1; D1.1, D3.1.
OUTG	Growth in real net output 1968–77, measured by index number of real net output 1977, base year 1968.
Sources:	F5, E1.1.
LABG	Growth in employment 1968–77, measured by index numbers of employment in 1977, base 1968.
Sources:	G5, E1.

Labour quality

PCF*	Females as a proportion of the workforce.
Sources:	C1, C4, E3.1, E3.2.
PART*	Part-time workers as a proportion of the workforce. For the United

Kingdom in 1977 direct observations are available in the Employment Census for that year; for 1968, the Census of Population (1971) was the best source: we define a part-time worker as one working fewer than 30 hours. For the United States in both years an indirect method was used: *PARTS* was estimated from data on total production-worker hours on the assumption that the average full-time worker works 2,000 hours annually, as opposed to 1,000 hours for the average part-time worker.

Sources: B2, C4; D1.1, D3.1.

NOPS*   Non-operatives as a proportion of the workforce.

Sources: A1.3, A3.2; D1.1, D3.1.

ED*   Average years of schooling of labour force (1971). This includes formal tertiary education (but not vocational training). This is measured by mean years for the United Kingdom, but median for the United States. For the United States, observations typically relate to more aggregate industry definitions than the 3-digit level.

Sources: B3, D4.1.

MGR   Managers and kindred occupations as a proportion of the workforce (1971). For the United States observations typically refer to more aggregate definitions than the 3-digit level.

Sources: B1, D4.2.

MGRRDK   is *MGR* × *RDK* (see below for definition of *RD*).

Labour relations

STRIK*   Average number of strikes per plant. For 1967/8 we used the average of 1971–3 (the nearest years for which sufficiently disaggregated data were available), and for 1977, the average of 1976–8. For the latter period in the United Kingdom, only more aggregate, roughly 2-digit data, were available: these were disaggregated within sectors on the assumption of similar *intra-sector* distributions as were observed for 1971–3.

Sources: A1.2, C2, A31, C5; E1, D1.1, E2, D3.1.

WDL   Proportion of working days actually worked, that is, the proportion of days *not* lost due to strikes. The years of observations and assumptions used in overcoming data deficiencies in the United Kingdom are as explained for *STRIK*.

Sources: A1.2, C2, A3.1, C5; E2.1, D1.1, E2.2, D3.1.

STCOV   Proportion of workforce involved in the average strike. This is derived as the ratio of the proportion of workers directly involved in strikes to the number of strikes per plant. The year of observations and assumptions used in overcoming data deficiencies in the United Kingdom are as explained for *STRIK*.

Sources: A1.2, C2, A3.1, C5; E2.1, D1.1, E2.2, D3.1.

UNION*   Proportion of workforce belonging to labour unions. For the United Kingdom the estimates are disaggregations to the MLH level of aggregate figures for sixteen broadly defined sectors (Bain and Price 1980) using information on the proportion of the workforce covered by collective bargaining agreements.

Sources: C3, C6, G1, G4.

BEL* An index of disharmony or bellicosity in labour relations. As explained in Chapter 3 pp. 38–9, the country constituents of this variable are measured as the estimated residuals from regressions (table 3.2) explaining strike intensity in each country in terms of plant size and various characteristics of the workforce.

Industry structure and related variables

AD (*) Advertising–sales ratio. For the United Kingdom, 1977 data are unavailable at the 3-digit level, and 1968 is used in its stead. For the United States, 1967 data were taken from the input–output table but 1976 data from a newly available source that is averaged where possible over 1973–6.

ADC (*) Advertising–sales ratio, but in consumer convenience-goods industries only.

Sources: A1.5, D7, F.

C5(*) Five-firm seller concentration ratios for sales. This is the weighted average of the 5-firm ratios for the principal products of the industry. For the United States these have been estimated, by interpolation, from the reported 4- and 8-firm ratios (see note 8 to Chapter 3).

Sources: A2.1, A4.1, D2.2, D3.3.

FOSK Proportion of industry sales in the United Kingdom accounted for by companies classified as foreign owned. These data are only available at a suitably disaggregated level for 1968.

Source: A1.4.

KBARR Capital stock of the typical size plant. Defined as $\log CAP + \log TP$.

REGS Average distance shipped within the United States for physical units of output classified to the American industry (used as an indicator of regionalisation in the United States).

Source: D5.

PF Number of plants operated by the five largest firms. This involves estimation by interpolation of size distributions for the United States, but not for the United Kingdom.

Sources: A1.6; A3.3; D2.2, D3.3.

RD (*) Expenditure on research and development as a proportion of industry sales. For the United Kingdom these data are available for only 35 separate industry classifications (1972, 1977). These have been disaggregated to the MLH level using Population Census data on the proportion of the workforce classified as scientists, engineers and technicians. The disaggregation is based on the assumption that R&D is distributed across MLHs within each aggregate industry in the same way as in the proportion of scientists, engineers and technicians. For the United States the data source used for

1967 is similarly aggregated; for 1977 we used a different source that provides more detail for the years 1974–6.

Sources: A4.2, A4.3, B3; F, G6.

SMAL   Incidence of small plants. Defined as the proportion of industry employment accounted for by plants employing fewer than 50 workers.

Sources: A1.1, A3.4; D1.2, D3.2.

VI   Vertical integration. This is proxied by the ratio of net output to gross output.

Sources: A1.2, A3.1; D1.1, D3.1.

Trade

IMEX(*)   Exposure to foreign competition, defined as the sum of imports and exports deflated by value of domestic market size (production + imports − exports).

IM(*)   Imports deflated by domestic market size.

EX(*)   Exports deflated by domestic market size.

COMP(*)   Trade adjusted concentration ratio. Defined for each country as:

$$COMP = C_5(1 + IMEX)^{-1}$$

All these variables can be computed in the United States for only 52 industries in 1967 and 59 in 1977 due to non-availability of comparable American trade data.

EXKD = EXK for British industries in which concentration exceeds the sample mean, and zero otherwise.

IMKD   *IMK* for British industries in which concentration exceeds the sample mean, and zero otherwise.

Sources;   A4.4, A4.5; D6.1, D6.2.

RAW   The degree to which an industry uses primary inputs (raw materials) among its inputs. This is measured as the sum of the input coefficients from the primary sectors as recorded in the American input–output tables.

Source: D7.

Wages and prices

PRICE   The ratio of UK/US unit values. For each industry, Smith, Hitchens and Davies (1982) computed from Census reports the ratio of UK/US average prices for as many comparable principal products as possible. These ratios were aggregated, using British quantity weights, to generate a price ratio for that industry. The price ratios for 1967/8 are those reported and discussed by Smith *et al*. The ratios for 1977 were computed for us by David Hitchens at the National Institute to whom we should like to express special thanks. In some industries, however, the selected products accounted for only a small proportion of total sales and/or were so broadly defined as to suggest that quality differences might render unit values potentially non-comparable. For our purposes such potentially heterogeneous products have been excluded, and this variable has been recomputed as the weighted average of the Smith *et al.* figures and the sample industry average value of *PRICE*, the weight being the coverage percentage of the remaining selected production in that industry's total sales.

WAGE   Average earnings per employee. Defined as total wage bill divided by employment (average number of employees over the year.)

Sources: A1.3, A3.2; D1.1, D3.1.

PROFIT   Labour share of value-added, derived from earlier defined variables by the identity

$$PROFIT \equiv PRICE^{-1} \times VPW^{-1} \times WAGE.$$

PRICEG   Growth in product price 1968–77 defined as the 1977 value of the index number for wholesale price (base year 1968).

Source: A4.6, E1.

WAGEG   Growth in wages 1968–77, defined as the ratio of *WAGE* in 1977 to *WAGE* in 1968.

KEY TO DATA SOURCES

UK government sources

A   Department of Trade and Industry, Business Statistics Office.

A1   *Report on the Census of Production, 1968* (London: HMSO, 1972)
1.   Vols. 8–141, table 2
2.   Vol. 156, table 1
3.   Vol. 156, table 2
4.   Vol. 158, table 44
5.   Vol. 156, table 4
6.   Vol. 158, table 42A

A2   *Report on the Census of Production, 1975* (London: HMSO, 1978)
1.   PA1009 Product Concentration of UK Manufactures, 1963, 1968 and 1975.

A3   *Report on the Census of Production, 1977*
1.   PA1002, table 1
2.   PA1002, table 2
3.   PA1002, table 13
4.   PA211–499, table 4

Other publications

A4   1.   PO1006 Statistics of Product Concentration of UK Manufactures for 1975, 1976 and 1977 (HMSO, 1980)
2.   Business Monitor MO14, Industrial Research and Development Expenditure and Employment (HMSO 1975)
3.   Business Monitor MO14, Industrial Research and Development Expenditure and Employment (HMSO 1978)

    4. Business Monitor MO12 Import Penetration and Export Sales Ratios for Manufacturing Industry, 1979
    5. Unpublished figures from BSO
    6. Trade and Industry 13/6/75 and 14/4/78 (supplemented by various editions of Annual Abstract, table 16.4 [HMSO])
B   Office of Population Censuses and Surveys
    Report on the Population Census 1971, Economic Activity
    1. Part III table 19
    2. Part IV table 26
    3. Qualified Manpower Tables
C   Department of Employment
    1. British Labour Statistics, Year Book 1972, table 5 (HMSO 1974)
    2. Department of Employment Gazette, Feb. 1976, pp. 115–126
    3. New Earnings Survey 1973 (HMSO 1974), tables 110, 111
    4. Census of Employment 1977
    5. Department of Employment Gazettes, June 1977, pp.579–86; June 1978, pp.690–9; July 1979, pp.661–70
    6. New Earnings Survey 1978 (HMSO 1978) tables 203,4.

US government sources

D   Department of Commerce
D1 Bureau of the Census, *1967 Census of Manufactures* (Government Printing Office, 1971)
    1. Vol. 2, *Industry Statistics* (Industry Reports, table 1a)
    2. Vol. 2, *Industry Statistics* (Industry Reports, table 4)
    3. Vol. 1, *Summary and Subject Statistics* (Chapter 2, table 3)
D2 Bureau of the Census, *1972 Census of Manufactures* (Government Printing Office, 1976)
    1. Vol. 2, *Industry Statistics* (Industry Reports, table 1a)
    3. Special Report Series, *Concentration Ratios in Manufacturing*, MC72(SR)–9 (tables 5, 6)
D3 Bureau of the Census, *1977 Census of Manufactures* (Government Printing Office, 1981)
    1. Vol. 2, *Industry Statistics* (Industry Reports, table 1a)
    2. Vol. 2, *Industry Statistics* (Industry Reports, table 4)
    3. Special Report Series, *Concentration Ratios in Manufacturing*, MC77(SR)–9 (table 5)
D4 Bureau of the Census, *Census of Population, 1970*
    1. Subject Reports, *Industrial Characteristics*, PC(2)–7B
    2. Subject Reports, *Occupation by Industry*, PC(2)–7C
D5 Bureau of the Census, *1972 Census of Transportation* (Government Printing Office, 1975)
D6 Bureau of the Census, *U.S. Commodity Exports and Imports as Related to Output*
    1. *1967* (Government Printing Office, 1969)
    2. *1977* (Government Printing Office, 1979)
D7 Bureau of Economic Analysis, *Input–Output Table for 1972* (data tape)

E   Department of Labor, Bureau of Labor Statistics
E1   Data tape containing indexes of prices, real output, productivity, and labour input, input–output industries (described in *Time Series Data for Input–Output Industries*, Bulletin No. 2018)
E2   *Analysis of Work Stoppages*
     1. Bulletin No. 1611 (Government Printing Office, 1969), table A–1
     2. Bulletin No. 2032 (Government Printing Office, 1979), table 14
E3   *Employment and Earnings*
     1. Vol. 15 (August 1968), table B–3
     2. Vol. 25 (March 1978), table B–3
F   Federal Trade Commission, Bureau of Economics, *Annual Line of Business Report, 1974–1976* (Federal Trade Commission, 1981–2)
G   Other sources
G1   Bain, G., and R. Price, *Profiles of Union Growth* (Oxford: Basil Blackwell, 1980), tables 2.8–2.23
G2   Elliott, I., 'Disaggregation of 1968 gross fixed capital stock data to MLH level – revision and testing of estimates' (mimeo; London: National Economic Development Office, 1976)
G3   Allard, R., 'Estimates of capital stock for manufacturing industry by MLH,' (mimeo.; 1982), based on investment data reported in Censuses of Production
G4   Freeman, R. B., and J. L. Medoff, 'New estimates of private sector unionism in the United States,' *Industrial and Labor Relations Review*, 32 (January 1968), 143–74
G5   Wenban-Smith, G., 'A study of the movement of productivity in individual industries in the United Kingdom,' *National Institute Economic Review*, No. 97 (August 1981), describes the data used, which are largely Business Statistics Office and Department of Employment index numbers
G6   National Science Foundation, *Research and Development in Industry, 1972*, NS 74–312 (Government Printing Office, 1974)

NOTES

1 PRODUCTIVITY LEVELS IN BRITISH AND AMERICAN INDUSTRIES

1 We quote 1970 rather than 1973 because the authors' calculations are based on a trans-national comparison in that year using purchasing-power exchange rates, which is then extended forward and backward in time by means of real output and input indices for each of the countries in the comparison.

2 The result indicating low 'quality' for German labour may be spurious for failing to take into account Germany's extensive system of vocational training outside the years of full-time schooling; see Prais and Wagner (1983).

3 Sapsford's (1981) figures are consistent with the United Kingdom's best catch-up performance preceding 1973. Martin (1984) fitted functions to annual data for 1960–80 to test the hypothesis that output per head for a number of European countries was catching up to that of the United States. One of the techniques that he used shows logistic convergence for all countries that he analysed except Britain (rapid for Netherlands, Belgium, Germany, and Japan; slow for France and Italy).

4 See the introduction to a symposium on Britain's comparative productivity, *National Institute Economic Review*, no. 101 (August 1982), pp. 9–12, for an early recognition. Maddison (1984) noted that the growth of the capital–labour ratio, an important driver of labour productivity, had dropped generally in the industrial countries in the 1970s, but the deceleration was less in Britain than in any but France.

5 Ulman (1968) provided a survey that emphasises these linkages between labour relations and the underlying structure of society and social attitudes.

6 Information summarised in Pratten and Atkinson (1976). Also see Prais (1981, pp. 104, 120, 215–16, 254–5).

7 Central Policy Review Staff (1975, p. 82); Pratten (1976, p. 52). According to the Central Policy Review Staff, British plants require up to twice as much time for rectifying faults as do continental plants (p. 84). Also, breakdowns of equipment cost twice as many hours as on the Continent, although in Britain identical machinery is maintained by 50 to 70 per cent more plant maintenance personnel.

8 Price Commission (1978, pp. 5, 28). Executives in selected industries have suggested that inventory holdings in some British industries may be inflated by 15 to 20 per cent (Caves, 1980, p. 147).

9 Most evidence bears on the motor industry. See Central Policy Review Staff (1975, pp. 24, 71, 75, 95–6).

10 Furthermore, an analysis of productivity in American affiliates and British domestic companies suggested that the American superiority in labour

productivity might result from concentration in the more capital-intensive industries.

11 Sociologists have explored the hypothesis that British management might be a self-perpetuating class which, presumably, would suffer in performance from excluding more able entrants from other family backgrounds. The evidence properly interpreted shows no support for this; see Poole *et al.* (1981) and earlier references cited therein.

12 Prais (1981, chaps. 14, 17) documented the pattern in case studies of machine tools and typewriters. Other statistical studies also suggest that due to quality differences British goods have given ground to competitors in both home and foreign markets (Brech and Stout, 1981).

13 The review of the Industrial Reorganisation Corporation's performance by Hague and Wilkinson (1983) gives it a good rating for the administrative efficacy of its promotion of mergers but expresses considerable scepticism about the normative objective itself.

14 *Fortune*, August 20, 1984, p. 213.

15 See George and Ward (1975, Chapter 5); Hughes (1976); and Pratten (1976).

16 See Firth (1979) on equity markets' evaluations of mergers in the United Kingdom and Meeks (1977), Cowling *et al.* (1980), and Prais (1981, pp. 177–9) for ex post evidence. Studies of stock-market valuations of mergers in the United States have, in contrast, invariably inferred significant average gains in market value for bidder and target firms taken together.

17 See Department of Trade and Industry (1971, p. 68). Figures for other countries are given (Belgium and France, 51 per cent; Japan, 54 per cent; Netherlands, 58 per cent; Australia, 60 per cent; Switzerland, 61 per cent; Italy, 66 per cent), but their comparability with the United Kingdom figure is less certain than for those quoted in the text.

18 See the exchange in *Journal of Industrial Economics*, 29 (March 1981), and references cited therein.

19 It is not clear, however, that other industrial countries would exhibit patterns that are very different.

2 RELATIVE INDUSTRIAL PRODUCTIVITY: AN ANALYTICAL FRAMEWORK

1 See Bloch (1974), Saunders (1980), Caves, Porter and Spence (1980, Chapter 10), and Bernhardt (1981) on Canada, and Caves (1984) on Australia.

2 The model described in the text is simplified, of course, in a number of respects, particularly in our choice of production function and the assumption of constant *intra*-industry capital intensity. It is not difficult conceptually to substitute more general production functions but we prefer not to do so for statistical reasons. For example, generalising to the CES production function and using Kmenta's linear approximation (1967) would imply an additional term in our estimating equation measuring the UK/US difference in the square of logged capital intensity. Since we would wish to allow for inter-country and sector differences in the parameters of the function, this term would bring with it a barrage of

additional variations as will become clear from the following subsection. Thus we persevere with the Cobb-Douglas in order to economise on degrees of freedom and so retain the flexibility we need when later testing hypotheses about the wide range of non-production function determinants of relative productivity.

The assumption that all plants within each industry have the same capital intensity can be relaxed by assuming inter-firm variations which are random and/or size related (Davies and Caves (1983), p. A9). The practical implications are that equation (6) remains appropriate so long as intra-industry variations in capital intensity are broadly similar in the two countries, and if capital intensity is correlated with size, the coefficient on TP will reflect this factor as well as the extent of returns to scale.

3 It would be equally valid to add $CAPS$ and TPS, rather than $CAPK$ and TPK. This would generate an identical overall fit and parameter estimates. In various places in the text we interpret higher (lower) α values as indicative of more (less) productive capital. This represents the fact that the marginal product of capital curve is higher at every L for given (A), the higher is α. We cannot, of course, directly equate α to capital productivity, which depends on the level of capital intensity as well as α.

4 Nevertheless, as a check, we undertook a series of experiments in which a variable measuring the UK/US difference in plant size dispersion was added to the equations reported in table 3.1. This variable proved consistently insignificant with a coefficient and t-value very close to zero. We measured $(1/2)\sigma^2$ by the log of the ratio of midpoint to mean plant size. In the case of a lognormal size distribution, this equals $(\mu + \sigma^2) - (\mu + (1/2)\sigma^2) = (1/2)\sigma^2$. But, more generally, it should still prove to be a fairly useful indicator of the degree of dispersion.

5 To see this, consider the extreme case where one characteristic is completely inclusive of another – that only workers exhibiting characteristic 1 can exhibit characteristic 2 (for example, only female workers are part-time, although not all female workers). In this case the expected value in efficiency units of a randomly selected worker is:

$$\{(1 - p_1) + \lambda_1(p_1 - p_2) + \lambda_1\lambda_2 p_2\}\{(1 - p_3 + \lambda_3 p_3\} \ldots$$

$$= \{1 + (\lambda_1 - 1)p_1 + \lambda_1(\lambda_2 - 1)p_2\} \prod_{j=3}^{c} \{1 + (\lambda_j - 1)p_j$$

Here, we require that $(\lambda_1 - 1)p_1 + \lambda_1(\lambda_2 - 1)p_2$ is 'small,' as well as the remaining $(\lambda_j - 1)p_j$. So long as this requirement is met, the resulting estimating equation remains as in the case of independent characteristics: there are c additional explanatory variables (that is, the $p_{Kj} - p_{Sj}$). But note that the coefficient on p_2 is now $\lambda_1(\lambda_2 - 1)$ rather than $\lambda_2 - 1$. Because all workers with characteristic 2 also have characteristic 1, the regression coefficient will reflect the effect of both characteristics on productivity.

6 This assumption is unlikely to hold in practice. If we substitute the empirically more realistic assumption that the number of strikes is proportionate to plant size, then it can be shown that N in (14) now refers to the Herfindahl equivalent number of plants. In our statistical research we experiment with both definitions of N.

7 Brown *et al.* (1981) suggested that only 40 per cent of one-day strikes are recorded in the United Kingdom.

3 DETERMINANTS OF RELATIVE EFFICIENCY

1 These matches are reported in Appendix 1.
2 Each variable not otherwise designated takes the form of a ratio of the British industry's observation to that for its American counterpart. In some cases a difference is taken, rather than a ratio, for reasons growing out of the theoretical model presented in Chapter 2. Variables pertaining just to the United Kingdom or United States are given symbols ending in K or S respectively. Detailed information on the sources of all variables is provided in Appendix II.
3 The relative-price deflators were based on the data on quantities and values of selected products that are given for most industries in each country's census (their calculation is explained fully in Smith, Hitchens, and Davies, 1982). However, in some industries these selected products accounted for a small proportion of total sales and, in such cases, it was feared that this might add considerable noise to our dependent variable. Therefore, we constructed the deflators ultimately used by forming a weighted average of the relative unit value for each industry and the average price deflator for the whole sample, the weight being the coverage percentage of the selected products listed in the census. This has the effect of dampening inter-industry variance and rendering our correction for relative price differences only a partial one.
4 The theoretical specification for these variables developed in Chapter 2 indicated that they should be entered into the regression model as differences between the British and American proportion and in unlogged form, whereas the estimating equation otherwise takes a logarithmic form.
5 The interpretation of the slope shift variables requires the addition of their coefficients to those of CAP and TP. As a check that the dummy slope variables are not merely picking up broad intersectoral differences, not necessarily specific to capital intensity or plant size, equation 3 was estimated with dummy intercept instead of dummy slope terms. The explained variance fell drastically.
6 The issue is in fact a bit complicated. A positive coefficient for MGR, like ED, simply indicates that adding more of an input that is not 'raw' labour increases the average productivity of raw labour. That conclusion itself establishes nothing about the actual relative to the optimal input of that factor which enhances labour's productivity. We take up that problem of inference later in this study.
7 On the other hand, the simple arithmetic adjustment to the labour input figures implicitly restricts the coefficient on WDL to be equal to that on labour (β in our production function framework).
8 Because data for the United States report concentration for the leading four firms, it was necessary to estimate American five-firm concentration by interpolation on the cumulative concentration curve. For 1967/8, for example, the average value of C_5S in our sample for that year was 14 points less than the average for C_5K. The correlation between them was only 0.59, less than

expected on the familiar evidence that concentration patterns are similar among industrial countries.

9 In general we expect that flows of imports and exports will also depend on productivity, and so the variable *IMEX* creates a potential problem of simultaneous-equations bias. We address this problem in Chapter 4. In the interim, though, we note that this variable suffers less markedly from the bias than would import and export shares taken separately. The hypothesis that we wish to test here takes the form

$$y = a + \beta z + u_1$$

with $\beta > 0$ expected where y is productivity and z is exposure to world competition. If we proxy z by m, import penetration, then:

$$m = \gamma + \delta y + u_2, \text{ with } \delta < 0 \text{ expected, so } E(u_1, m) \neq 0.$$

Similarly for export performance, x,

$$x = \epsilon + \varphi y + u_3, \text{ with } \varphi > 0 \text{ expected, so } E(u_1, x) \neq 0.$$

However, measuring z by $x + m$, the relation running from y to z (and thus u_1) should be weaker.

10 Prais (1981, Chapter 2) suggested that Germany's small-plant population is definitely larger than Britain's, and that of the United States seems proportionally no smaller. In our sample the means of *SMALK* and *SMALS* are almost identical, respectively 13.4 and 13.9 per cent. However, the correlation between them, 0.68, is not particularly high.

11 The case studies in Prais (1981, pp. 107, 143–44, 153–55) shed some light on this hypothesis.

12 In 1977 the frequency of the strikes in the United Kingdom is highly correlated with both wage levels (0.345) and producer concentration (0.474). The pattern is similar in the United States (0.466 and 0.460 respectively).

13 If *BEL* is simply deleted from the 1967/8 model (the final version presented in table 3.4 below), the value of R^2 declines only from 0.50 to 0.48, and other coefficients show no appreciable changes. That is, if one chooses conservatively to give up *BEL* as a bad try, our other conclusions are unaffected.

4 PRODUCTIVITY, PRICES, MARKET STRUCTURE, AND INTERNATIONAL TRADE

1 This relationship may run through relative prices (low productivity results in high domestic prices and therefore a non-competitive status in international trade), although the traditional theory of international trade stresses the determination of relative prices in the world economy outside the (small) nation, in which case differences between domestic and foreign prices will not be observed.

2 We note a change from Chapter 3 in the measurement of *SIZE*. There we measured the variable as an average of relative total industry sales and relative total industry employment. That *ad hoc* procedure was intended to blunt the simultaneity involved in including *SIZE* as a regressor in the ordinary least

squares model of *VPW*. Now that protection is no longer needed, therefore, for the statistical analysis of this chapter we measure it simply by relative sales.

3 In estimating this relationship we took account (to no avail) of the hypothesis that the effect of relative R & D expenditures might be conditional on the relative extent of foreign direct investment in Britain.

4 Although many foreign investments have been made as responses to trade restrictions, the tendency for mature multinational companies to supply markets from their lowest-cost source worldwide and to secure components processed overseas at a lowest-cost location seems to have established a positive net relationship between foreign investment and trade, at least for mature industrial countries such as Britain (see Davies and Hughes, 1985) and the United States (Bergsten, Horst, and Moran, 1978).

5 With typical plant size controlled, the effect of trade exposure should be chiefly through its effect on numbers of plants and multiplant operation. Export opportunities and import competition affect the former in opposite directions and have no evident relation to the latter.

6 This result suggests a useful statistical project to analyse the comparative sizes of the small-business in industries matched between the United Kingdom and other countries. A study by White (1982) provides a starting point. Not too much should be made of the high t-statistic of *SMAL*, because it and the dependent variable are estimated from the same plant-size distributions.

7 The variable *AD* here has been modified by multiplying it by a dummy that equals one for consumer convenience-good industries, zero otherwise.

8 *KBARR*, the comparative capital assets of the typical-size plant, is defined as log $CAP + \log TP$. *ADC* was explained in note 7.

9 This result is consistent with the interpretation that we gave to the influence of *PRICE* on *IMEXK* in table 4.1.

5 RELATIVE PRODUCTIVITY IN LARGE PLANTS

1 The ratio Y_1/Y_2 (or its inverse) has been widely used in other contexts as a proxy for the slope of the cost curve and the economies of scale that it reflects. Although the ratio also reflects many other factors, not least the degree to which small units in an industry are less capital-intensive than their larger competitors, the empirical evidence consistently indicates that the ratio's variance among industries does contain some evidence on their relative scale economies. See Caves, Khalilzadeh-Shirazi, and Porter (1975) and Caves and Pugel (1980).

2 For 1967/8 the sample mean of w (0.5195) indicates that Y_2S/Y_1S, the cost disadvantage ratio, equals 0.925 on average, that is, in the average American industry small plants suffer a labour-productivity disadvantage of 7.5 per cent relative to the large ones. For 1977 the disadvantage appears to be 11 per cent.

3 The same conclusion emerges clearly if we examine correlations in each country between the median size of plants and the productivity of large relative to small plants. In 1977 the correlation between *TPS* and Y_1S/Y_2S is 0.461, whereas the correlation for the corresponding British variables is -0.087; in 1967/8 the values are 0.473 and -0.099.

4 Caves and Pugel (1980) confirmed this for the United States. They found that the variation of capital intensity with size seems to reflect underlying technology, and that the slope of the capital intensity/size relation in turn affects the size distribution of firms and the performance levels of large and small firms in predictable ways.

6 RELATIVE PRODUCTIVITY GROWTH

1 This proposition was put forth as a reflection on the British economy by Caves and others (1968, pp. 487–95) and was developed into a sweeping socioeconomic model by Olson (1982).

2 In Caves and others (1968, pp. 261–3, 274).

3 They found that the coefficient of variation of labour-productivity growth rates during this period was 0.49 in Britain, only 0.29 in Germany. For total factor productivity the corresponding values were 0.90 and 0.57.

4 The correlations between the British and American magnitudes are 0.545 for output growth and 0.249 for employment.

5 A statistical strengthening also occurred, since Wragg and Robertson reported corrected R^2 values of 0.39 and 0.52 for their two periods.

6 The objection to using the mean in cross-section is the prominent influence it assigns to economically unimportant differences between industries in the numbers of very small plants. That problem is eliminated by leaving out the smaller plant-size classes.

7 The shifts expressed in terms of the American variables obtain somewhat higher t-statistics than if British variables are used.

8 Conceivably, the shedding of previously hoarded labour could be associated with rapid productivity growth, but most British manufacturing industries did not appear to seize that initiative during the period of our study.

9 This is an example of how our research design scores over traditional inter-industry studies of productivity growth within a single country (for example, Wragg and Robertson, 1978). In such studies inter-industry differences in the potential for technical progress (essentially unmeasurable) have the effect of introducing a considerable amount of random noise. In our study, innate differences in potential cancel out when the UK/US ratio is employed.

10 Equation (3) is similar, but not identical, to the Gompertz and logistic diffusion curves, treating A_K as the level of diffusion and A_S as the saturation level (which itself changes). Perhaps a more helpful way of expressing (3) is as

$$A_{1K}/A_{oK} = (A_{1S}/A_{oS}) * (A_{oK}/A_{oS})^{b-1} \tag{3a}$$

Thus if A_{1S}/A_{oS} reflects the movement of best practice (assuming that the United States is always at the frontier), then this affects technical progress in the United Kingdom (A_{1K}/A_{oK}). But the United Kingdom can grow faster than the best-practice *rate* by catching up $(b < 1)$, or it might slip further behind $(b > 1)$.

11 Log $EFF \equiv \log VPW_{1968} - \Sigma\beta_i X_i$ where X_i are the core variables in 1968 and β_i their estimated coefficients as defined in our best overall equation for 1967/8. Thus log EFF is not strictly the same as the ordinary least squares residuals, having a mean of -0.294. Similarly, log $EFFG \equiv \log VPWG - \Sigma\gamma_i Z_i$ where the

γ_i and ζ_i refer to a regression equation equivalent to equation (5) in table 6.4, but excluding *EFF* as an explanatory variable. It has a mean of -0.164.

12 The proof of this statement is that $\log EFFG \equiv \log (A_{1K}/A_{1S}) - \log (A_{oK}/A_{oS})$ and $\log EFF \equiv \log (A_{oK}/A_{oS})$. Thus, if $-\log EFF = \log EFFG$, then $\log (A_{1K}/A_{1S}) = 0$ and $A_{1K} = A_{1S}$.

13 The industries whose MLH numbers appear in chart 6.1 are: 216, sugar; 221, edible oils and fats; 272, pharmaceuticals; 276, plastics materials; 411, manmade fibres; and 450, footwear. Notice that they represent (excepting footwear) the sort of process industries not subject to the conjunction of managerial and labour-relations difficulties that on our evidence pose the main barrier to British productivity.

7 CONCLUSIONS AND POLICY IMPLICATIONS

1 This chapter is written so as to be accessible to those who have not toiled through all the technical details of Chapters 2–6. Therefore, specific technical connections between those and the present chapter will be confined to footnotes.

2 We do not imply that A- and B-type factors are qualitatively different from one another. It is simply a matter of whether economic theory and available data suffice to manoeuvre a factor into the A category. Those factors that remain stubbornly in the B category may interact with the identified A elements, complicating the interpretation of the A-type effects that we have identified as well as creating statistical problems for the estimation procedure.

3 This indicator of disharmony in industrial relations, *BEL*, is the zero-meaned residuals from a regression equation explaining strike activity. Since *BEL* is the UK/US difference, it too has a zero mean (see the second section of Chapter 3).

4 So long as our comparative observations on each variable accurately reflect inter-industry variance, any constant scale or unit difference between the British and American data will not affect the regression coefficient on the variable concerned.

5 This is because *ED* refers to arithmetic mean years of schooling in the United Kingdom but median years in the United States. Since the distribution of schooling within an industry is likely to be positively skewed, the mean will typically exceed the median. In that case equally educated workforces in the two countries correspond to a positive value of *ED* as defined. Note, however, that this does not affect the variance of *ED* so long as the relationship between median and mean is fairly stable across industries.

6 The two data sources differ with respect to deflation, and furthermore we cannot be sure that identical accounting conventions have been used to draw up both sets of capital stock estimates.

7 In terms of notation used above, these are the variables *CAP* (and *CHECAP*, *ELCAP*, and *BMCAP*), *BEL*, *TPK*, and *IMEXK*.

8 One can conceive this as the weighted average of four alternative intercepts corresponding to the four sectors differentiated by the dummy slope variables. To compute these, we substitute not the overall sample means for *CHECAP*, *ELCAP*, *BMCAP*, but rather the mean of only the non-zero observations on

each variable (that is, the mean value of CAP for the industries in each sector). The weighted average of these figures therefore refers to the expected productivity gap which would occur for a randomly selected industry with the probabilities of its being selected from these different sectors given by their sample frequencies.

9   These are antilogarithms; the model was estimated in logarithmic form.

10   Bearing in mind our doubts that a zero value for ED indicates rather less than equality, the figure shown may even understate the true effect of a move to equality in the educational input. On the other hand, since we suspect that $PART$ reflects the influence of factors other than part-time working *per se*, the figure of 8.8 per cent shown in table 7.4 should be treated cautiously.

11   In this particular sector, and not in common with the general sample experience, our estimates indicate much smaller typical plant sizes (by 42 per cent) on average in the United Kingdom than in the United States. We therefore interpret a move to equality as an increase in British plant size. But this invalidates our assumption of constant TPK, hence the adjustment.

12   The 58 per cent increase refers to a hypothetical, randomly selected, industry with only a small probability (about 10 per cent) that it will be selected from electrical and instrument engineering. Thus the overall contribution of equality in $ELTP$ is a weighted average of 19 per cent and zero.

13   $UNION$ and $NOPS$ now have no effect because their regression coefficients were not found to be significantly different from zero, and these variables have been excluded from our best equation.

14   On the reasonable assumption that an explanatory variable displays an approximately normal sample distribution, roughly 16 per cent of the sample industries will record observations in excess of this so-called best practice. As a numerical example, the sample mean and standard deviation of log CAP for 1967/8 are -0.928 and 0.570. Thus we contemplate the effects of increasing relative capital intensity by rather more than 50 per cent. This best-practice level is exceeded by 10 of the sample industries.

15   Two points of detail concerning the derivation of this predicted value should be mentioned. First, since the effect of an improvement in capital intensity varies among sectors, we have used a weighted average of the regression coefficients on the CAP variables. Second, while a move to best practice concerning TPK requires a reduction in plant size, via $ELTP$ it requires an increase for those industries in electrical and instrument engineering. Therefore, we have posited a decrease in plant size in all industries not in that sector, for which an increase has been assumed. Accordingly, the contribution from industries within EL has been calculated net of the adverse effect of increasing TPK.

16   The lower gain estimated from 1977 data to result from a shift to best practice results in part from the exclusion in 1977 of the variables $UNION$ and $NOPS$. It is also due to the reduced impact of TPK, which is offset (ironically) by the significance of TP that obtains in 1977 but not 1967/8.

17   Without recourse to what might be unjustified assumptions concerning the payment of factors.

18   We have given thought to the implication that our results may reveal that the United States uses too much of an input, say, rather than that Britain uses too

little. When we place the conclusions that we obtained against the general reservoir of evidence on efficiency problems in the American economy, we conclude that we have not erred in placing the shoes on British feet.

19 As we indicated in Chapter 1, this proposition depends on the nation's production structure not already being fully adjusted to the productivity-depressing factors that have been identified. No formal evidence is at hand, without cross-section analyses farther apart in time than our decade interval permits. However, the sentence that follows in the text is, we believe, a reasonable reading of the evidence.

20 See the evidence on Sweden in Carlsson (1972), on Australia in Caves (1984), and on Canada in Caves, Porter, and Spence (1980) and Harris (1984).

REFERENCES

Aitchison, A. and Brown, J., 1957, *The Lognormal Distribution*, Cambridge University Press

Aylen, J., 1982, 'Plant size and efficiency in the steel industry: an international comparison', *National Institute Economic Review*, no. 100, May, pp. 65–76

Bain, G. and Price, R., 1980, *Profiles of Union Growth*, Oxford, Basil Blackwell, tables 2.8–2.23

Baldwin, J.R. and Gorecki, P.K., 1983, 'Trade, tariffs, product diversity and length of production run in Canadian manufacturing industries: 1970–79', Economic Council of Canada, Discussion Paper no. 247

Bergsten, C.F., Horst, T. and Moran, T.H., 1978, *American Multinationals and American Interests*, Washington, Brookings Institution

Bernhardt, I., 1981, 'Sources of productivity differences among Canadian manufacturing industries', *Review of Economics and Statistics*, vol. 63, November, pp. 503–12

Bloch, H., 1974, 'Prices, costs, and profits in Canadian manufacturing: the influence of tariffs and concentration', *Canadian Journal of Economics*, vol. 7, November, pp. 594–610

Brech, M.J. and Stout, D.K., 1981, 'The rate of exchange and non-price competitiveness: a provisional study within U.S. manufactured exports', *Oxford Economic Papers*, vol. 33 (supplement, July), pp. 269–81

Brown, C. and Medoff, J., 1978, 'Trade unions in the production process', *Journal of Political Economy*, vol. 86, June, pp. 355–78

Brown, W. *et al.*, 1981, *The Changing Contours of British Industrial Relations: A Survey of Manufacturing Industry*, Oxford, Basil Blackwell

Carlsson, B., 1972, 'The measurement of efficiency in production: an application to Swedish manufacturing industries', *Swedish Journal of Economics*, vol. 74, pp. 468–85

Caves, R.E., 1974, 'Multinational firms, competition, and productivity in host-country industries', *Economica*, vol. 41, May, pp. 176–93

Caves, R.E., 1980, 'Productivity differences among industries', in Caves, R.E. and Krause, L.B. (eds), *Britain's Economic Performance*, Washington, Brookings Institution, pp. 135–92

Caves, R.E., 1981, 'Intra industry trade and market structure in the industrial countries', *Oxford Economic Papers*, vol. 33, July, pp. 203–23

Caves, R.E., 1984, 'Scale, openness, and productivity in manufacturing industries', in Caves, R.E. and Krause, L.B. (eds), *The Australian Economy: A View from the North*, Washington, Brookings Institution, pp. 313–47

Caves, R.E. and Associates, 1968, *Britain's Economic Prospects*, Washington, Brookings Institution

Caves, R.E., Khalilzadeh-Shirazi, J. and Porter, M.E., 1975, 'Scale economies in statistical analyses of market power', *Review of Economics and Statistics*, vol. 57, May, pp. 133–40

Caves, R.E., Porter, M.E. and Spence, A.M., 1980, *Competition in the Open Economy: A Model Applied to Canada*, Cambridge, Harvard University Press

Caves, R.E. and Pugel, T.A., 1980, Intraindustry differences in conduct and performance: viable strategies in U.S. manufacturing industries, Monograph series in Finance and Economics, no. 1980–2, New York, Graduate School of Business Administration, New York University.

Central Policy Review Staff, 1975, *The Future of the British Car Industry*, London, HMSO

Chandrasekar, K., 1973, 'US and French productivity in 18 manufacturing industries', *Journal of Industrial Economics*, no. 21, pp. 110–25

Christensen, L.R., Cummings, D. and Jorgenson, D.W., 1981, 'Relative productivity levels, 1947–1973: an international comparison', *European Economic Review*, vol. 16, May, pp. 61–94

Cockerill, A. and Silberston, A., 1974, *The Steel Industry: International Comparisons of Industrial Structure and Performance*, University of Cambridge, Department of Applied Economics, Occasional Paper 42, Cambridge University Press

Connell, D., 1979, *The UK's Performance in Export Markets: Some Evidence from International Trade Data*, London, National Economic Development Office

Cowling, K. *et al.*, 1980, *Mergers and Economic Performance*, Cambridge University Press

Creigh, S.W. and Makeham, P., 1978, 'Foreign ownership and strike-proneness: a research note', *British Journal of Industrial Relations*, vol. 16, November, pp. 369–72

Crockett, G. and Elias, P., 1984, 'British managers: a study of their education, training, mobility, and earnings', *British Journal of Industrial Relations*, vol. 22, March, pp. 34–46

Daems, H., 1985, 'The size of the firm: theoretical and empirical reflections on European industrial hierarchies', unpublished manuscript, Catholic University of Leuven

Daly, A., 1982, 'The contribution of education to economic growth in Britain: a note on the evidence', *National Institute Economic Review*, no. 101, August, pp. 48–56

Daly, A., Hitchens, D.M.W.N. and Wagner, K., 1985, 'Productivity, machinery and skills in a sample of British and German manufacturing plants: results of a pilot enquiry', *National Institute Economic Review*, no. 111, February, pp. 48–61

Davies, S.W. and Caves, R.E., 1983, 'Inter-industry analysis of United Kingdom–United States productivity differences', National Institute of Economic and Social Research, Discussion paper no. 61

Davies, S.W. and Hughes, K.S., 1985, 'Multinationals and the trade balance: the U.K. experience', University of East Anglia, Working paper

Department of Trade and Industry, 1971, *Report of the Committee of Inquiry on Small Firms*, Cmnd 4811, HMSO

Downie, J., 1958, *The Competitive Process*, London, Butterworths

Dunning, J.H., 1970, *Studies in International Investment*, London, George Allen and Unwin

Dunning, J.H. and Pearce, R.D., 1977, *U.S. Industry in Britain: An Economists Advisory Group Research Study*, Boulder, CO, Westview Press

Elliott, I. and Hughes, A., 1976, 'Capital and labour: their growth, distribution and productivity', in Panić, M. (ed.), *UK and West German Manufacturing Industry, 1954–72: A Comparison of Structure and Performance*, NEDO Monograph no. 5, London, National Economic Development Office, pp. 15–50

Farrell, M.L., 1957, 'The measurement of productive efficiency', *Journal of the Royal Statistical Society*, Series A, vol. 120 (part III), pp. 253–66

Firth, M., 1980, 'The profitability of takeovers and mergers', *Economic Journal*, vol. 89, June, pp. 316–28

Florence, P. Sargant, 1972, *Logic of Industrial Organisation* (3rd edn), London, Routledge and Kegan Paul

Forsyth, D.J.C., 1973, 'Foreign-owned firms and labour relations: a regional perspective', *British Journal of Industrial Relations*, vol. 11, March, pp. 20–28

Frankel, M., 1957, *British and American Manufacturing Productivity: A Comparison and Interpretation*, Bureau of Economic and Business Research, University of Illinois, Bulletin no. 81, Urbana, University of Illinois Press

George, K.D. and Ward, T.S., 1975, *The Structure of Industry in the EEC*, University of Cambridge, Department of Applied Economics, Occasional Paper no. 43, Cambridge University Press

Globerman, S., 1979, 'Foreign direct investment and 'spillover' efficiency benefits in Canadian manufacturing industries', *Canadian Journal of Economics*, vol. 12, February, pp. 42–56

Griliches, Z. and Ringstad, V., 1971, *Economies of Scale and the Form of the Production Function: An Econometric Study of Norwegian Manufacturing Establishment Data*, Amsterdam, North-Holland Publishing Company

Hague, D. and Wilkinson, G., 1983, *The IRC – An Experiment in Industrial Intervention*, London, George Allen and Unwin

Hannah, L. and Kay, J., 1977, *Concentration in Modern Industry*, London, Macmillan

Harris, R., 1984, 'Applied general equilibrium analysis of small open economies with scale economies and imperfect competition', *American Economic Review*, vol. 74, December, pp. 1016–32

Hart, P.E. and Clarke, R., 1980, *Concentration in British Industry, 1935–75*, National Institute of Economic and Social Research, Occasional Paper no. 32, Cambridge University Press

Houseman, S.N., 1985, Job security and industrial restructuring in the European Community steel industry, Ph.D. dissertation, Harvard University

Hughes, A., 1976, 'Company concentration, size of plant, and merger activity', in Panić, M. (ed.) *The UK and West German Industry, 1954–72: A Comparison of Structure and Performance*, NEDO Monograph no. 5, London, National Economic Development Office, pp. 75–115

Jones, D.T., 1976, 'Output, employment and labour productivity in Europe since 1955', *National Institute Economic Review*, no. 77, August, pp. 72–85

Kendall, M.G., 1961, 'Natural law in the social sciences', *Journal of the Royal Statistical Society* (Series A), vol. 124 (Part 1), pp. 1–16

Kmenta, J., 1967, 'On the estimation of the C.E.S. production function', *International Economic Review*, vol. 8, pp. 180–9

Kumar, M.S., 1985, 'Growth, acquisition activity and firm size: evidence from the United Kingdom', *Journal of Industrial Economics*, vol. 33, March, pp. 327–3

Leslie, D., 1976, 'Hours and overtime in British and United States manufacturing industries: a comparison', *British Journal of Industrial Relations*, vol. 14, July, pp. 194–201

Maddison, A., 1977, 'Phases of capitalist development', *Banca Nazionale del Lavoro Quarterly Review*, no. 121, June

Maddison, A., 1984, 'Comparative analysis of the productivity situation in the advanced capitalist countries', in Kendrick, J.H. (ed.), *International Comparisons of Productivity and Causes of the Slowdown*, Cambridge, Ballinger

Marginson, P.M., 1984, 'The distinctive effects of plant and company size on workplace industrial relations', *British Journal of Industrial Relations*, vol. 22, March, pp. 1–14

Martin, S., 1984, 'Convergence as an empirical determinant of long-run productivity growth', Birkbeck College, Discussion paper no. 158

Meeks, G., 1977, *Disappointing Marriage: A Study of the Gains from Merger*, University of Cambridge, Department of Applied Economics, Occasional Paper no. 51, Cambridge University Press

National Board for Prices and Incomes, 1970, 'Hours of work, overtime and shift working', Report 161, *Cmnd* 4554, HMSO

Nelson, R.R. and Winter, S.G., 1978, 'Forces generating and limiting concentration under Schumpeterian competition', *Bell Journal of Economics*, vol. 9, Autumn, pp. 524–48

Olson, M., 1982, *The Rise and Decline of Nations: Economic Growth, Stagflation, and Social Rigidities*, New Haven, Yale University Press

Owen, N., 1983, *Economics of Scale, Competitiveness, and Trade Patterns within the European Community*, Oxford University Press

Paige, D. and Bombach, G., 1959, *A Comparison of National Output and Productivity in the United Kingdom and the United States*, Paris, Organisation for European Economic Cooperation, chapter 5

Pavitt, K. (ed.), 1980, *Technical Innovation and British Economic Performance*, London, Macmillan

Phelps-Brown, H., 1977, 'What is the British predicament?', *Three Banks Review*, no. 116, December, pp. 3–29

Poole, M. *et al.*, 1981, *Managers in Focus: The British Manager in the Early 1980s*, Aldershot, Gower Publishing Company

Prais, S.J., 1976, *The Evolution of Giant Firms in Britain*, Cambridge University Press

Prais, S.J., 1978, 'The strike-proneness of large plants in Britain', *Journal of the Royal Statistical Society* (Series A), vol. 141, part 3, pp. 368–8

Prais, S.J., 1981, *Productivity and Industrial Structure*, Cambridge University Press

Prais, S.J. and Wagner, K., 1983, 'Some practical aspects of human capital investment: training standards in five occupations in Britain and Germany', *National Institute Economic Review*, no. 105, August, pp. 46–65

Pratten, C.F., 1976, *Labour Productivity Differentials within International Companies*, Cambridge University Press

Pratten, C.F. and Atkinson, A.G., 1976, 'The use of manpower in British manufacturing industry', *Department of Employment Gazette*, no. 84, June, pp. 571–6

Price Commission, 1978, *Metal Box Ltd – Open Top Food and Beverage and Aerosol Cans*, HC 135, HMSO

Pryor, F.L., 1972, 'Size of establishments in manufacturing', *Economic Journal*, vol. 82, June, pp. 547–66

Ray, G.F., 1984a, 'Changes in industrial structure', *National Institute Economic Review*, no. 107, February, pp. 50-3

Ray, G.F., 1984b, *The Diffusion of Mature Technologies*, National Institute of Economic and Social Research, Occasional Paper no. 36, Cambridge University Press

Rostas, L., 1948, *Comparative Productivity in British and American Industry*, National Institute of Economic and Social Research, Occasional Paper no. 13, Cambridge University Press

Roy, A.D., 1982, 'Labour productivity in 1980: an international comparison', *National Institute Economic Review*, no. 101, August, pp. 26–37

Sapsford, D., 1981, 'Productivity growth in the UK: a reconsideration', *Applied Economics*, vol. 13, December, pp. 499–512

Saunders, R., 1980, 'The determinants of productivity in Canadian manufacturing industries', *Journal of Industrial Economics*, vol. 29, December, pp. 167–84

Scherer, F.M., 1975, *The Economics of Multi-Plant Operation: An International Comparisons Study*, Cambridge, Harvard University Press

Smith, A.D. and Hitchens, D.M.W.N., 1983, 'Comparisons of British and American productivity in retailing', *National Institute Economic Review*, no. 104, May, pp. 45–57

Smith, A.D., Hitchens, D.M.W.N. and Davies, S.W., 1982, *International Industrial Productivity: A Comparison of Britain, America and Germany*, National Institute of Economic and Social Research, Occasional Paper no. 34, Cambridge University Press

Smith, D.C., 1980, 'Trade union growth and industrial disputes', in Caves, R.E. and Krause, L.B. (eds), *Britain's Economic Performance*, Washington, Brookings Institution, pp. 81–134

Solomon, R.F. and Ingham, K.P.D., 1977, 'Discriminating between MNC subsidiaries and indigenous companies: a comparative analysis of the British mechanical engineering industry', Oxford *Bulletin of Economics and Statistics*, vol. 39, May, pp. 127–38

Steuer, M.D. and Gennard, J., 1971, 'Industrial relations, labour disputes and labour utilization in foreign-owned firms in the United Kingdom', in Dunning, J.H. (ed.), *The Multinational Enterprise*, London, George Allen and Unwin, chapter 4

Swann, D. *et al.*, 1974, *Competition in British Industry: Restrictive Practices Legislation in Theory and Practice*, London, Allen and Unwin

Turk, C., 1984, 'Strike activity and uncertainty', London School of Economics, Centre for Labour Economics, Discussion paper no. 205

Ulman, L., 1968, 'Collective bargaining and industrial efficiency', in Caves, R.E. and Associates, *Britain's Economic Prospects*, Washington, Brookings Institution, pp. 324–80

Utton, M., 1982, 'Domestic concentration and international trade', *Oxford Economic Papers*, vol. 34, November, pp. 479–97

Wenban-Smith, G.C., 1981, 'A study of the movements of productivity in individual industries in the United Kingdom 1968–79', *National Institute Economic Review*, no. 97, August, pp. 57–66

West, E.G., 1971, *Canada–United States Price and Productivity Differences in Manufacturing Industries, 1963*, Ottowa: Economic Council of Canada

White, L.J., 1982, 'The determinants of the relative importance of small business', *Review of Economics and Statistics*, vol. 64, February, pp. 42–9

Williams, K., Williams, J. and Thomas, D., 1983, *Why Are the British Bad at Manufacturing?*, London, Routledge and Kegan Paul

Wragg, R. and Robertson, J., 1978, *Post-War Trends in Employment, Productivity, Output, Labour Costs and Prices by Industry in the United Kingdom*, Department of Employment, Research paper no. 3, London, HMSO

Yukizawa, E., 1975, *Japanese and American Productivity*, Kyoto Institute of Economic Research

INDEX

advertising intensity, 54, 55, 56, 58
Atkinson, A.G., 112n
Aitchison, A., 22
Aylen, J., 13

Baldwin, J.R., 58
barriers to entry, 56, 59
bellicosity, 29, 38, 45–7, 49, 55–6, 58, 62–3, 68–70, 79, 80
    see also labour relations
Bergsten, C.F., 117n
Bernhardt, I., 113n
Bloch, H., 113n
Bolton Committee, 13
Bombach, G., 17
Brech, M.J., 113n
Brown, C., 40
Brown, J., 22
Brown, W., 115n

capital input per head, 2–3
capital intensity, 20–1, 32–4, 46, 49, 54, 56, 58–9, 62, 68–9, 80, 84–5, 87–8, 90–3
capital-labour ratio, 18, 20
Carlsson B., 121n
catch-up, 2–3, 25–6, 37, 71, 77–8, 80–3
Central Policy Review Staff, 7, 8
Chandrasekar, K., 17
Christensen, L.R., 2
Clarke, R., 14
Cockerill, A., 13
collusion, 40
competition, 21, 35, 40–1, 47, 91, 94
    see also international trade
concentration, 14, 21, 40–1, 46, 52, 56, 59, 62, 63
Connell, D., 11
Cowling, K., 113n
Creigh, S.W., 9
Crockett, G., 10
Cummings, D., 2

Daems, H., 12
Daly, A., 10, 11
diffusion, 77–8
Downie, J., 40

Dunning, J.H., 9

economies of scale, 14, 17, 32–3, 35, 41–2, 49, 70, 79, 83, 85, 89
education, 10
    vocational, 10, 33, 96–7
    years of schooling, 33, 35, 58, 68, 84, 88–9
efficiency, 7, 11, 14, 16, 18–20, 24, 35, 40–1, 43, 46, 63, 77–8, 81, 83
Elias, P., 10
Elliott, I., 73
exports, competition in, 15, 41, 51, 53–4, 59–63, 68, 87
    see also international trade

Farrell, M.L., 92
Firth, M., 113n
foreign-controlled industries, 36, 41, 44, 56, 58, 60, 63, 79
Forsyth, D.J.C., 9
Frankel, M., 17

Gennard, J., 9
George, K.D., 12, 13, 113n
Globerman, S., 80
Gorecki, P.K., 58
Griliches, Z., 33

Hague, D., 113n
Hannah, L., 21
Harris, R., 14, 42, 58, 121n
Hart, P.E., 14
Herfindahl index, 21
Hitchens, D.M.W.N., 3, 4, 10, 115n
Horst, T., 117n
Houseman, S.N., 95
Hughes, A., 13, 73, 113n
Hughes, K.S., 117n
human capital, 8, 10–11, 17, 23, 33, 35, 49, 86, 89, 91, 94–5, 96

imports, competition in, 15, 41, 51, 53–4, 56, 59–63, 68, 79, 87
    see also international trade
industry size, 43, 47, 54, 62
inflation rate, 5

Ingham, K.P.D., 9
international trade, competition in, 11, 13, 41,
    50–2, 55, 59, 62–3, 84, 88
    see also imports *and* exports

Jones, D.T., 3
Jorgenson, D.W., 2

Katrak, H., 11
Kay, J., 21
Kendall, M.G., 28
Khalilzadeh-Shirazi, J., 117n
Kmenta, J., 113n
Kumar, M.S., 12

labour costs, 15
labour input, 2–3, 20, 37
labour productivity in manufacturing, 3, 4, 6,
    17ff, 32
labour relations, 4–8, 9, 14, 24–30, 32, 37–8,
    44–7, 49, 63, 70, 80, 83–4, 88, 91, 93–4
    see also bellicosity
Leslie, D., 7

Maddison, A., 3, 112n
Makeham, P., 9
managerial factors, 4, 7–11, 35–7, 43–4, 49, 69,
    79–80, 83, 93, 95
Marginson, P.M., 5, 8
market size, 52, 56, 62, 63
Martin, S., 71, 112n
Medoff, J., 40
Meeks, G., 113n
mergers, 12, 14
Moran, T.H., 117n

National Board for Prices and Incomes, 7
National Training Survey, 10
Nelson, R.R., 59

Olson, M., 15, 118n
output per head, 2–3, 5, 13, 17, 25, 31, 84ff, 91
overtime, 6–7
Owen, N., 14

Paige, D., 17
Pavitt, K., 36
Pearce, R.D., 9
Phelps Brown, H., 15
plant size,
    comparisons of, 4, 5, 8–9, 11–14, 18–21,
        32–3, 35, 41–2, 44–5, 49, 52–4, 58–63, 75,
        84–5, 87–91
    measurement of, 13, 21–2
Poole, M., 113n
Porter, M.E., 113n, 117n, 121n

Prais, S.J., 5, 8, 10, 14, 28, 29, 38, 93, 112n,
    113n
Pratten, C.F., 6, 8, 112n, 113n
Price Commission, 8
production function, 17–21, 23, 25, 31–2, 42,
    49, 78
profitability, 53, 56, 59, 60, 62
Pryor, F.L. 13
Pugel, T.A., 117n, 118n

Ray, G.F., 14, 15
relative productivity,
    growth of, 71–83
    in large/small plants, 64–70
research and development, 36–7, 44, 54–6,
    58–9, 68, 79, 84–5, 89–91, 93
restrictive labour practices, 6, 15, 35, 39
Ringstad, V., 33
Robertson, J., 74, 118n
Rostas, L., 17
Roy, A.D., 3

Sapsford, D., 112n
Saunders, R., 113n
Scherer, F.M., 58
skill levels,
    differences in, 33, 35, 96
    investment in, 10, 14
    see also education
Smith, A.D., 3, 4, 5, 115n
Solomon, R.F., 9
Spence, A.M. 113n, 121n
Steuer, M.D., 9
Stout, D.K., 113n
strikes, 5, 24, 38, 69
    costs of, 25–7, 37–8, 46
    'knock-on' effects of, 37–8, 45
Swann, D., 40

Thomas, D., 15
total factor productivity, 2–3, 15, 92
trade union membership, effects on labour
    relations, 6, 15, 38–40, 45, 62–3, 69,
        79–80, 83, 91, 95
Turk, C., 5

Ulman, L., 112n
Utton, M., 41

Verdoorn's Law, 42, 50, 62, 74

Wagner, K., 10, 112n
Ward, T.S., 12, 13, 113n
Wenban-Smith, G., 74
West, E.G., 17

White, L.J., 117n
Wilkinson, G., 113n
Williams, J., 15
Williams, K., 15
Winter, S.G., 59
workforce,
    proportion of females in, 33, 35, 38–9, 58,
        69, 89–90, 91

proportion of non-production workers in, 33,
    35, 38–9, 54, 55, 60, 68, 90, 91
proportion of part-timers in, 33, 35, 38–9,
    58, 89–90
Wragg, R., 74, 118n

Youth Training Scheme, 97
Yukizawa, E., 17

THE NATIONAL INSTITUTE OF ECONOMIC
AND SOCIAL RESEARCH
PUBLICATIONS IN PRINT

published by
THE CAMBRIDGE UNIVERSITY PRESS
(available from booksellers, or in case of difficulty from the publishers)

ECONOMIC AND SOCIAL STUDIES

XIX   *The Antitrust Laws of the USA: A Study of Competition Enforced by Law*
By A.D. NEALE and D.G. GOYDER. 3rd edn. 1980. pp. 548. £40.00 net.

XXI   *Industrial Growth and World Trade: An Empirical Study of Trends in Production, Consumption and Trade in Manufactures from 1899–1959 with a Discussion of Probable Future Trends*
By ALFRED MAIZELS. Reprinted with corrections, 1971. pp. 563. £22.50 net.

XXV   *Exports and Economic Growth of Developing Countries*
By ALFRED MAIZELS assisted by L.F. CAMPBELL-BOROSS and P.B.W. RAYMENT. 1968. pp. 445. £20.00 net.

XXVII *The Framework of Regional Economics in the United Kingdom*
By A.J. BROWN. 1972. pp. 372. £22.50 net.

XXVIII *The Structure, Size and Costs of Urban Settlements*
By P.A. STONE. 1973. pp. 304. £18.50 net.

XXIX   *The Diffusion of New Industrial Processes: An International Study*
Edited by L. NABSETH and G.F. RAY. 1974. pp. 346. £22.50 net.

XXXI   *British Economic Policy, 1960–74*
Edited by F.T. BLACKABY. 1978. pp. 710. £40.00 net.

XXXII *Industrialisation and the Basis for Trade*
By R.A. BATCHELOR, R.L. MAJOR and A.D. MORGAN. 1980. pp. 380. £30.00 net.

XXXIII *Productivity and Industrial Structure*
By S.J. PRAIS. 1982. pp. 410. £30.00 net.

XXXIV *World Inflation since 1950. An International Comparative Study*
By A.J. BROWN assisted by JANE DARBY. 1985. pp. 428. £30.00 net.

OCCASIONAL PAPERS

XXXI   *Diversification and Competition*
By M.A. UTTON. 1979. pp. 124. £19.50 net.

XXXII *Concentration in British Industry, 1935–75*
By P.E. HART and R. CLARKE. 1980. pp. 178. £23.50 net.

XXXIV *International Industrial Productivity*
By A.D. SMITH, D.M.W.N. HITCHENS and S.W. DAVIES 1982. pp. 184. £19.50 net.

XXXV   *Concentration and Foreign Trade*
By M.A. UTTON and A.D. MORGAN. 1983. pp. 150. £19.50 net.

XXXVI *The Diffusion of Mature Technologies*
By GEORGE F. RAY. 1984. pp. 96. £17.50 net.

XXXVII *Productivity in the Distributive Trades. A Comparison of Britain, America and Germany*
By A.D. SMITH and D.M.W.N. HITCHENS 1985. pp. 160. £19.50 net.

XXXVIII *Profits and Stability of Monopoly*
By M.A. UTTON. 1986. pp. 102. £12.95 net.

XXXIX *The Trade Cycle in Britain, 1958–1982*
by ANDREW BRITTON. 1986. pp. 108. £12.95 net.

NIESR STUDENTS EDITION

2. *The Antitrust Laws of the U.S.A.* (3rd edition, unabridged)
   By A.D. NEALE and D.G. GOYDER. 1980. pp. 548. £15.00 net.
4. *British Economic Policy, 1960–74: Demand Management* (an abridged version of *British Economic Policy, 1960–74*)
   Edited by F.T. BLACKABY. 1979. pp. 472. £11.95 net.
5. *The Evolution of Giant Firms in Britain* (2nd impression with a new preface)
   By S.J. PRAIS. 1981. pp. 344. £10.95 net.

THE NATIONAL INSTITUTE OF ECONOMIC AND SOCIAL RESEARCH

publishes regularly

THE NATIONAL INSTITUTE ECONOMIC REVIEW

A quarterly analysis of the general economic situation in the United Kingdom and overseas, with forecasts eighteen months ahead. The last issue each year usually contains an assessment of medium-term prospects. There are also in most issues special articles on subjects of interest to academic and business economists.

Annual subscriptions, £45.00 (home), and £60.00 (abroad), also single issues for the current year, £12.50 (home) and £18.00 (abroad), are available from NIESR, 2 Dean Trench Street, Smith Square, London, SW1P 3HE.

Subscriptions at the special reduced price of £18.00 p.a. are available to students in the United Kingdom and Irish Republic on application to the Secretary of the Institute.

Back numbers and reprints of issues which have gone out of stock are distributed by Wm. Dawson and Sons Ltd., Cannon House, Park Farm Road, Folkestone. Microfiche copies for the years 1959–84 are available from E P Microform Ltd., Bradford Road, East Ardsley, Wakefield, Yorks.

Published by

HEINEMANN EDUCATIONAL BOOKS

(distributed by Gower Publishing Company and available from booksellers).

THE UNITED KINGDOM ECONOMY
By the NIESR. 5th edition. 1982. pp. 119. £2.25 net.

DEMAND MANAGEMENT
Edited by MICHAEL POSNER. 1978. pp. 256. £6.50 net.

DE-INDUSTRIALISATION
Edited by FRANK BLACKABY. 1979. pp. 282. £12.95 (paperback) net.

BRITAIN IN EUROPE
Edited by WILLIAM WALLACE. 1980. pp. 224. £8.50 (paperback) net.

THE FUTURE OF PAY BARGAINING
Edited by FRANK BLACKABY. 1980. pp. 256. £16.00 (hardback), £7.50 (paperback) net.

INDUSTRIAL POLICY AND INNOVATION
Edited by CHARLES CARTER. 1981. pp. 250. £18.50 (hardback), £7.50 (paperback) net.

THE CONSTITUTION OF NORTHERN IRELAND
Edited by DAVID WATT. 1981. pp. 233. £19.50 (hardback), £9.50 (paperback) net.

RETIREMENT POLICY. THE NEXT FIFTY YEARS
Edited by MICHAEL FOGARTY. 1982. pp. 224. £17.50 (hardback), £7.50 (paperback) net.

SLOWER GROWTH IN THE WESTERN WORLD
Edited by R.C.O. MATTHEWS. 1982. pp. 182. £19.50 (hardback), £9.50 (paperback) net.

NATIONAL INTERESTS AND LOCAL GOVERNMENT
Edited by KEN YOUNG. 1983. pp. 180. £17.50 (hardback), £9.50 (paperback) net.

EMPLOYMENT OUTPUT AND INFLATION
Edited by A.J.C. BRITTON. 1983. pp. 208. £25.00 net.

THE TROUBLED ALLIANCE. ATLANTIC RELATIONS IN THE 1980s
Edited by LAWRENCE FREEDMAN. 1983. pp. 176. £19.50 (hardback), £7.50 (paperback) net.

EDUCATION AND ECONOMIC PERFORMANCE
Edited by G.D.N. WORSWICK. 1984. pp. 152. £18.50 net.

Published by
GOWER PUBLISHING COMPANY LTD

ENERGY SELF-SUFFICIENCY FOR THE UK
Edited by ROBERT BELGRAVE and MARGARET CORNELL. 1985. pp. 224. £19.50 net.

THE FUTURE OF BRITISH DEFENCE POLICY
Edited by JOHN ROPER. 1985. pp. 214. £18.50 net.

ENERGY MANAGEMENT: CAN WE LEARN FROM OTHERS?
By GEORGE F. RAY. 1985. pp. 131. £19.50 net.

UNEMPLOYMENT AND LABOUR MARKET POLICIES
Edited by P.E. HART. 1986. pp. 230. £19.50 net.

NEW PRIORITIES IN PUBLIC SPENDING
Edited by M.S. LEVITT. 1987. pp. 136. £17.50 net.